THE STRUCTURED LITERACY PLAYBOOK

Preplanned Lessons for Building Phonics and Fluency Skills

MELISSA ORKIN, SARAH GANNON,
AND ALEXANDRIA OSBURN
FOREWORD BY MARYANNE WOLF

Produced for DK by
BookLife Publishing
OMNI House, King's Lynn, Norfolk PE30 4LS

Authors
Melissa Orkin, PhD
Sarah Gannon, MEd
Alexandria Osburn, MSEd

DK LONDON
Senior Editor Amelia Jones
Project Art Editor Anna Scully
Managing Editor Katherine Neep
Managing Art Editor Sarah Corcoran
Senior Production Editor Andy Hilliard
Senior Production Controller Meskerem Berhane
Publisher Sarah Forbes
Managing Director, Learning Hilary Fine

First published in Great Britain in 2025 by
Dorling Kindersley Limited
20 Vauxhall Bridge Road,
London SW1V 2SA

The authorised representative in the EEA is
Dorling Kindersley Verlag GmbH. Arnulfstr. 124,
80636 Munich, Germany

25 26 27 28 29 10 9 8 7 6 5 4 3 2 1
001-350064-Sep/2025

A CIP catalogue record for this book
is available from the British Library.
ISBN: 978-0-2417-5301-9

Printed and bound in China

www.dk.com

This book was made with Forest Stewardship Council™ certified paper – one small step in DK's commitment to a sustainable future.
Learn more at www.dk.com/uk/information/sustainability

Contents

Foreword by Maryanne Wolf

In the ever-evolving field of literacy education, there is one shared goal among teachers, regardless of their particular method of teaching: that is, to enable every child to read and to understand that learning to read will give each of them a whole new world, a world where they can become their best selves. The authors of this book integrate the best of our field's theoretical knowledge and their many years of teaching experience to help every teacher teach every child. That said, there is an ongoing challenge faced by teachers today. How do they effectively meet the diverse needs of young learners, all the while adhering to evidence-based practices?

The Structured Literacy Playbook rises to this challenge, offering educators a practical and transformative approach to primary school literacy intervention. This book provides more than just guidance; it delivers a comprehensive framework for planning and delivering targeted instruction. By integrating pre-planned lessons aligned with the phases of word reading development, *The Structured Literacy Playbook* equips teachers with tools that bridge the gap between research and classroom practice. Each lesson goes beyond the surface of phonics instruction, embedding word reading strategies into meaningful literacy experiences that foster fluency, vocabulary growth and comprehension. My own work on the new RAVE-O intervention programme is based on what we have called the POSSUM approach. POSSUM is an acronym that stands for Phonology (sounds), Orthography (spelling), Semantics (vocabulary and its connections), Syntax (grammar), Understanding (comprehension) and Morphology (morphemes) and highlights a multi-component approach that develops, integrates and automatises knowledge across multiple aspects of word knowledge (Orkin et al, 2022; Wolf & Katzir-Cohen, 2001).

Principles from this work are incorporated in this book's wonderful ways of emphasising the multiple components that go beyond phonics and that contribute to fluency and deep reading. One of the greatest gifts in the teaching profession is to watch how what we teach becomes part of the next generation's contributions. Dr Melissa Orkin, one of the authors of this book, did her PhD with me and continues to conduct work with me, particularly on fluency. I could not be prouder of what she has achieved and of what she and her co-authors have done in this book that will reach far more teachers than I ever could.

Designed specifically with educators in mind, the structure of *The Structured Literacy Playbook* reflects a deep understanding of classroom realities. Organised by increasingly complex phonics concepts, its chapters progress methodically, ensuring that each new strategy builds on previous knowledge. From continuous blending techniques for early readers in Chapter 1 to exploring multiple-meaning words in later chapters, the content evolves alongside pupils' developmental needs.

What sets *The Structured Literacy Playbook* apart is its seamless integration of foundational literacy elements with engaging, decodable texts from Phonic Books. Through a teacher-friendly format, it pairs clear, concise rationales for instructional routines with vibrant, well-illustrated examples. The inclusion of a QR code to access supplemental lesson materials ensures that educators have the resources they need at their fingertips.

At its core, *The Structured Literacy Playbook* recognises that literacy is not just about decoding words, but also about understanding and using the multiple aspects of language effectively. Each lesson addresses a cohesive set of skills – phonics, sight word recognition, vocabulary, morphology, fluency, comprehension and spelling – offering a holistic approach that supports oral and written language development.

Whether you are a seasoned educator looking to refine your practice or a newcomer seeking a structured path to literacy instruction, *The Structured Literacy Playbook* provides the insight, strategies and resources to empower your teaching. It is more than a book – it is a guide to unlocking the potential of every young reader, one word at a time.

Maryanne Wolf is the Director of the Center for Dyslexia, Diverse Learners, and Social Justice at UCLA and has authored over 170 scientific publications and books, including Proust and the Squid: The Story, Tales of Literacy for the 21st Century *and* Reader, Come Home. *She is co-author of the RAN/RAS naming speed tests and the creator of the RAVE-O intervention programme for all striving readers.*

A proud teacher, Maryanne Wolf (left), and her doctoral pupil, Melissa Orkin (right). (2013)

Introduction

The Structured Literacy Playbook offers instructional strategies and lesson frameworks for practical, sequential and efficient literacy development. Just as athletes require a balance of clear instruction and meaningful drills, pupils require support in developing their literacy skills. This book provides resources for educators to support skill development through thoughtful modelling, practice and coaching. Each chapter focuses on a **Game Plan**, a Structured Literacy routine that functions as a model lesson, which is designed to accompany a decodable text. The high-leverage instructional routines that comprise each Game Plan are referred to as **Winning Strategies** due to the empirical evidence that supports their efficacy. Game Plans can be delivered to a variety of pupils in both small group and tutorial formats and can be modified to fit different practice schedules. **Example Practice Schedules** feature pacing guides for lesson delivery and take into consideration the requirements for skill consolidation and incremental learning.

While there are other established intervention approaches that may support teaching certain key literacy skills and strategies at different points, the multi-componential approach described in this book aligns with current literacy research. Regardless of the curriculum used for phonics instruction, the evidence-based strategies highlighted in this text were selected to enhance the resources and educational strategies used by all literacy educators.

Support for Educators

One of the most rewarding experiences as a primary school educator is building literacy skills in young pupils. Research shows that literacy is fundamental for all other academic achievement (Hudson et al, 2021), yet ensuring expected progress among the majority of pupils remains a challenge. Three-quarters of schools in England identify poor attendance and low reading levels as primary obstacles affecting the academic progress of socio-economically disadvantaged pupils (The Education Endowment Foundation, 2025). The COVID-19 pandemic has exacerbated these issues, leading to significant learning losses; most children were estimated to have lost half a year of face-to-face schooling, impacting literacy development (National Literacy Trust, 2025; Sibieta, 2021).

Furthermore, disparities in literacy rates between different regions, such as the north-south divide, continue to persist, highlighting the need for targeted interventions to bridge these gaps (Green, 2025). Collectively, these factors underscore the pressing need for comprehensive strategies to address the multifaceted challenges hindering literacy achievement across the UK. The benefit of equipping educators with research-based tools and strategies has been evidenced by reading proficiency statistics, especially in the light of reading loss incurred as a result of COVID-19 (Picton, 2023). Overall, UK reading proficiency numbers are showing improvements since strategies such as the Phonics Screening Check and the English Hub were introduced (Department for Education, 2023). This tentative growth indicates the importance of high-leverage systems and practices for preventing "reading failure ... in all but a small percentage of children with serious learning disorders" (Moats, 2020).

Scientific Research Around Reading Instruction

Within the body of scientific literacy research, the following five major tenets are asserted:

1) Reading is unnatural (Wolf, 2007).

2) All children need some degree of explicit classroom instruction in fundamental literacy skills (phonemic awareness, phonics, fluency, vocabulary and comprehension) (National Reading Panel (US), 2000).

3) Pupils who demonstrate risk for reading impairment require additional targeted instruction through small group intervention or tutoring (Gersten et al, 2020; Wanzek et al, 2018).

4) Literacy instruction that maximises "explicit" pedagogical principles results in higher engagement and greater skill development (Archer & Hughes, 2011).

5) Targeted interventions that follow a Structured Literacy approach and integrate instruction on multiple aspects of word knowledge (i.e. phonics, vocabulary, morphology, syntax and comprehension) result in significant gains in reading achievement (Donegan & Wanzek, 2021; Lovett et al, 2014; Morris et al, 2012).

Creating Practical Resources

This book has been developed to address the challenges that teachers experience. Our observations of literacy instruction span multiple decades and various locations in public schools, private schools, clinical settings and research settings. Collectively, we have served as literacy coaches, classroom teachers, researchers and clinical directors and, regardless of our position, we have witnessed dedicated, well-intentioned, bright teachers struggle to achieve their literacy goals because of the complexity of reading development. This book's Game Plans were developed to reduce the demands on teachers and employ high-leverage practices that support pupils as they embark into lifelong learning. Game Plans can be used by a wide range of practitioners, including general educators, specialists, paraprofessionals and tutors.

Structured Literacy Instruction

One of the most promising findings in recent years has been the documented efficacy of Structured Literacy routines in efficiently developing foundational accuracy, fluency and comprehension skills (Fletcher et al, 2018; Foorman et al, 2016; National Reading Panel (US), 2000). Structured Literacy is an instructional approach characterised by teaching that is explicit, systematic and incremental, and integrates multiple aspects of word knowledge. Each pedagogical element of Structured Literacy has a strong body of empirical support.

Explicit instruction is considered a primary tool for ensuring equity among all pupils (Archer & Hughes, 2011). Teachers who use an explicit approach do not make assumptions about pupils' existing knowledge and provide clear models, offer plentiful opportunities for practice and deliver immediate corrective feedback to ensure efficient learning. Explicit instruction features a high level of pupil engagement through streamlined teacher language and embedded strategies. These strategies are designed to maximise whole group participation and include choral responses and paired conversations.

Systematic and Incremental Instruction

Systematic and incremental instruction ensures that skills are taught in a meaningful sequence that progresses from simple to complex. An incremental approach introduces skills individually, and lessons are crafted to include continual review, which builds skills in a cumulative manner.

Teaching Multiple Aspects of Word Knowledge

Integrating multiple aspects of word knowledge into a Structured Literacy routine implies delivering instruction that connects phonemic awareness and phonics strategies to other aspects of linguistic information, such as vocabulary, parts of speech and morphology. Literacy instruction that is multi-componential results in greater achievements than instruction that focuses on a single component (for example, phonemic awareness in isolation) (Donegan & Wanzek, 2021). There are several specialised, evidence-based intervention programmes that have demonstrated effective outcomes teaching pupils all aspects of word knowledge (Lovett et al, 2014; Morris et al, 2012). Notable among them is the RAVE-O programme (Wolf, 2011) originally developed by Maryanne Wolf and colleagues at the Tufts University Center for Reading and Language Research as a multi-componential approach for supporting reading fluency and comprehension at the primary school level. The RAVE-O programme influenced both the lesson frameworks and instructional routines embedded in this book's Game Plans. The curriculum and its documented efficacy inspired our instructional choices for small group intervention. Of particular note, the curriculum emphasises the importance of simultaneous instruction in efficient word recognition strategies, vocabulary development and activities that build knowledge about parts of speech and morphology.

Evidence-Based Theories That Emphasise the Multiple Aspects of Word Knowledge

The power of multi-componential instruction lies in the coordinated activation of all language areas involved in the reading process. Nearly all of the most widely supported theories of reading development acknowledge the integrated nature of both word reading and language comprehension.

These include the Simple View of Reading, which places equal importance on the contributions of decoding and language comprehension in reading comprehension (Gough & Tunmer, 1986), and the Reading Rope (Scarborough, 2001), which posits reading achievement as the result of language and decoding skills that become progressively more intertwined as pupils develop literacy abilities. Finally, the Four-Part Processing Model (Seidenberg & McClelland, 1989) is also rooted in the connectivist approach. It describes the interactive nature of multiple aspects of language knowledge, including phonological (sounds), orthographic (letter patterns), semantic (word meaning) and context in reading development.

Cognitive Evidence That Emphasises the Multiple Aspects of Word Knowledge

Our neurological understanding of reading development strengthens and expands earlier theoretical models. Nicknamed "the Reading Circuit", neuroscientists have identified groups of working neurons that become deeply interconnected as reading skills develop (Dehaene, 2010; Wolf, 2017).

Unlike innate abilities, such as language processing, reading is not hardwired into the brain; it must be learnt and constructed by repurposing existing neural systems for vision, language and cognition. This reading circuit involves areas responsible for decoding letters and sounds (phonology), recognising common letter patterns (orthography), activating word meanings (semantics), understanding parts of speech (syntax) and deciphering the ways in which morphemes (prefixes, suffixes and roots) impact pronunciation and meaning (Wolf, 2017). To build fluency, it is critically important to develop automaticity (the ability to effortlessly read words without having to decode them) within and across each cognitive aspect of word knowledge (Benjamin & Gaab, 2012; Wolf & Katzir-Cohen, 2001).

The Role of Phonics Skills

Phonics has been well established as a critical element in reading instruction (National Reading Panel (US), 2000). Phonics describes the system by which sounds are represented by letters and letter patterns in writing. The English language largely follows rules about when to use different letter patterns to spell English sounds. Approximately 50 per cent of English words follow these rules, and an additional 37 per cent of words contain only one sound-based exception. In order to read and spell proficiently, it is necessary for pupils to learn the phonics rules and practise their direct application (National Reading Panel (US), 2000). The purpose of phonics skills is to develop automatic word recognition, in which pupils can automatically and instantaneously retrieve most words. Automatic word retrieval is a significant contributor to overall reading fluency and comprehension. This skill emerges in phases that are facilitated by explicit, systematic instruction, as described in the following section.

Developing Word Recognition Skills

There are several predictable phases of word recognition, originally theorised by Linnea Ehri (1995), which describe how children progress from non-readers to readers with automatic word recognition. This book's chapters are organised in a sequence that complements pupils' development of word recognition skills, beginning with the Partial Alphabetic Phase. They mirror the sequence of word recognition development while simultaneously featuring high-utility phonics skills.

Phase 1 – Pre-Alphabetic: Pupils have not learnt the phonic code and "read" words by visual cues and memorisation. Most "reading" occurs with common logos or environment print (print that is seen in everyday life, such as street signs). For example, words such as "open", "exit" and "stop".

Phase 2 – Partial Alphabetic/Letters and Sounds: Pupils learn to decipher and manipulate the sounds in language, including matching letters to their corresponding sounds. In order to become proficient in the alphabetic principle, even for a handful of letters, pupils require instruction in complementary activities such as phonemic awareness tasks, knowledge of letter names, knowledge of letter sounds and letter formation. However, knowledge of letter sounds in isolation is limited and, in order to read, pupils must move to the next skill involved in word recognition – decoding.

Phase 3 – Full Alphabetic/Decoding: In the decoding phase of word recognition, pupils use their emerging knowledge of grapheme-phoneme correspondences to "sound out", or decode, words. A key skill in this phase involves the ability to maintain the accurate sequence of sounds while blending them together to pronounce a word – for example, the ability to accurately sequence the sounds /s/ /t/ /u/ /n/ /t/ and to correctly pronounce the word "stunt" instead of saying "stun" or "nuts". It is important to note that pupils do not need to know all the vowel sounds before they move to blending sounds together. Decoding can begin with one vowel sound and a handful of common consonants.

Phase 3.5 – Partial Mapping: This additional phase is not part of Ehri's original theory; however, conceptualising a midpoint from decoding to orthographic mapping can be helpful for instructional planning. The jump from decoding words to recognising them instantaneously can be challenging for many pupils. Incorporating techniques that support partial mapping is useful for moving pupils away from labour-intensive sound-by-sound reading and towards more efficient word recognition. By teaching pupils to recognise larger units or word parts, such as the rime pattern in a word (e.g. fit, dot, clap, held, ripe, scorn, beast), educators support greater efficiency in reading as pupils move to sight word recognition (Kilpatrick, 2020).

Reading by Rime Pattern

Reading words by rime pattern involves directing pupils to pronounce the rime pattern before pronouncing the entire word. Although it seems counterintuitive to read starting with the middle letters in a word, decoding by rime pattern offers several advantages. The first advantage is that the rime pattern stabilises the pronunciation of the vowel. Consider the ways in which the letter 'o' is pronounced in the following words: "go", "got" and "gown". The vowel pronunciation varies because the rime pattern indicates the word's syllable type. See Chapter 5 (pages 119–120) for more about the syllable type categories. The word "go" is an open syllable, and the vowel 'o' makes a long sound. The word "got" is a closed syllable, and the vowel 'o' makes a short sound. Finally, the word "gown" is a vowel diphthong, and the vowel 'o' combines with the letter 'w' to make a new vowel sound.

The pronunciation of the rime pattern activates a critical cue in our auditory memory. Evidence suggests that words are stored in our auditory memory by both initial sound and rime pattern. It is more difficult to retrieve a word when activating our memory for the vowel in isolation (Kilpatrick, 2020).

Phase 4 – Consolidated Alphabetic/ Orthographic Mapping: Word recognition development concludes with the ability to automatically pronounce the entire word without decoding. The cognitive process that underlies our sight word knowledge is called orthographic mapping. Once a word has been mapped, it functions as an "old friend" and is instantly recognisable across texts.

Defining Sight Words and Heart Words

Sight words are any words that are recognised and read automatically, meaning that they do not need to be sounded out, or decoded. (Sight words vary from pupil to pupil, depending on which words have been mapped for automatic recognition.) Most sight words are also considered high-frequency words. That is to say that they are commonly occurring in text (e.g. people, the, of, because). Many high-frequency words follow regular phonics spelling patterns, but some might be irregularly spelt.

Heart words are high-frequency words that contain one or more irregular spelling patterns (e.g. said, was, there). The heart word approach emphasises using traditional sound-spelling relationships and denotes any irregular spelling patterns with a heart symbol. When a word with advanced phonics patterns is introduced to younger pupils, we often discuss the notion of a "temporary heart word", meaning spelling patterns may seem irregular, but in later lessons pupils will learn the phonetic rule. For example, Reception pupils will likely need to read and spell "like". While "like" is phonetically regular and follows the split vowel spelling pattern, most commercial phonics programmes do not introduce this pattern until Year 1. Educators can follow the same protocol for teaching both temporary and permanent heart words.

The Cycle of Word Recognition

The phases of word recognition are not finite, but iterative. Early in their reading career, pupils learn short vowel sounds and most consonants, then move through the phases of word recognition for short vowel words. As a broader range of phonics rules are introduced, pupils begin again with Phase 2 of word recognition. The speed at which pupils move through the phases is typically faster once they have mapped short vowel sounds or closed syllable words.

Integrating Vocabulary, Syntax and Comprehension

Key areas of the reading circuit that are often overlooked during interventions include vocabulary, syntax and comprehension processes. Developing vocabulary knowledge includes not only increasing the number of words pupils know, but also strengthening the depth of knowledge they possess about each word, known as their "semantic neighbourhood" (Buchanan et al, 1996). Words with more associations live in a larger neighbourhood. The size of a semantic neighbourhood is positively associated with word recognition, with larger neighbourhoods facilitating faster word recognition (Pexman et al, 2002). Successful vocabulary instruction not only introduces pupils to new words but also supports the development of robust associations. Teachers can employ active processing strategies that connect word meaning to pupils' experiences through questioning techniques, use of visual supports and expanded dialogues (Beck et al, 2013).

Syntax refers to the system used to combine words in meaningful ways to create phrases and sentences. Knowledge of syntax includes parts of speech, grammar and punctuation. Although syntax is often associated with writing instruction, syntactic skills also support reading fluency and comprehension. The ability to identify key phrases in a sentence (e.g. subject, predicate and prepositional phrases) helps with automaticity, pacing and expression. Additionally, syntactic processes bridge word recognition to comprehension.

The ultimate goal of word recognition instruction is to facilitate fluent comprehension of texts. Although decodable texts are limited in their use of varied and complex language, opportunities to monitor comprehension are still available. Game Plan activities such as vocabulary instruction, sentence reading and morphology practice all reinforce comprehension at the single word and sentence level. Story-level comprehension is supported through questions that address pupils' understanding of lexical knowledge (the meaning of words in text), factual knowledge (the ability to retrieve information) and inferential analysis (connecting clues from the text with background knowledge to understand and reason).

The Backwards Planning Approach

Each Game Plan not only relies on a Structured Literacy framework but was also developed utilising a backwards planning approach. In backwards planning, the lesson is developed from a decodable book in order to target specific phonics skills. Educators might select the book based on the phonics progression of skill building used by their classroom curriculum, or they may use a diagnostic tool to identify areas that require remediation in small group or Wave 2 intervention. Backwards planning involves excerpting sentences and single words for reading, spelling and vocabulary practice. At times, additional words that provide practice with the targeted skills are supplemented to the lesson. Each chapter provides a roadmap titled **Planning for Game Day** which offers a sequence of steps to backwards plan the type of lesson being modelled.

Chapter Phonics Progression

Chapter 1: Beginning Decoding aligns with the Partial Alphabetic Phase and features instruction that supports blending sounds. Typically considered a mid- to late-Reception skill, blending sounds accurately while reading is critical for early word recognition. Chapter 2: Developing Automaticity with Simple Decoding moves pupils beyond the continuous blending of individual sounds by introducing rime pattern instruction. This phase of word recognition is referred to as Partial Mapping and is characterised by the ability to recognise "chunks" of letters, such as the rime pattern.

The next two chapters support pupils' automatic word recognition as they encounter longer words. In Chapter 3: Early Sight Word Development, instruction guides pupils in efficiently recognising words that include final adjacent consonants. Chapter 4: Building Stamina with Longer Words continues to enhance recognition skills with words that begin with adjacent consonants or digraphs. Chapter 5: Decoding Multisyllabic Words introduces pupils to strategies for dividing and efficiently decoding multisyllabic words with closed vowel sounds. Although educators often lament the significant proportion of time allocated to short vowel phonics patterns, it is important to keep in mind the utility of this knowledge. Short vowel patterns are the most common of all syllable types in English and provide pupils with strategies to decode approximately 40 per cent of all words in the language (Stanback, 1992).

Although spelling activities are integrated into every chapter, Chapter 6: Spelling Strategies with Suffixes pays special attention to the connection between decoding and encoding. The chapter offers instructional strategies for teaching spelling generalisations when adding suffixes. Spelling with suffixes is a common challenge in primary school and can bottleneck fluency with written expression.

Chapter 7: Decoding New Vowel Sounds, the final chapter, features instruction on automatic word recognition with long vowel words that contain a split vowel spelling (also known as final silent 'e' or vowel-consonant-e). Once pupils have orthographically mapped the two most common syllable types (closed and split vowel), they should be able to command approximately 50 per cent of English words (Stanback, 1992).

Phonics Progression of *The Structured Literacy Playbook*

Chapters	Phonics Concept	Example Words	Additional Aspects of Word Knowledge
Chapter 1: Beginning Decoding	Continuous Blending of Single-Syllable Two- and Three-Letter Short Vowel Words (VC and CVC)	it, sit, at, sat	Integration of Vocabulary Instruction
Chapter 2: Developing Automaticity with Simple Decoding	Rime Pattern Recognition of Two- and Three-Letter Short Vowel Words (VC and CVC)	map, cap, sad, mad	Irregular Word/Heart Word Instruction
Chapter 3: Early Sight Word Development	Rime Pattern Recognition of Four-Letter Short Vowel Words with Final Adjacent Consonants (CVCC)	bunk, junk, best, rest	Use of RAN Charts Developing Associations to Vocabulary Words
Chapter 4: Building Stamina with Longer Words	Recognition of Four- and Five-Letter Short Vowel Words with Initial Adjacent Consonants or Digraphs (CCVC and CCVCC); Suffix -s	trust, crust	Exploring Multiple-Meaning Word Vocabulary
Chapter 5: Decoding Multisyllabic Words	Reading and Spelling Multisyllabic Words with Short Vowel Syllables; Syllable Division; Suffix -s/-es	sandpit, muffin	Practising Spelling Rules for Suffix -s and -es
Chapter 6: Spelling Strategies with Suffixes	Spelling Strategies for Single- and Multi-Syllable Short Vowel Words with Suffixes -ed and -ing	scanned, grabbed, mittens	Understanding the Purpose of Common Suffixes Exploring Parts of Speech and Phrasing in Sentences
Chapter 7: Decoding New Vowel Sounds	Rime Pattern Recognition of Split Vowel Spelling Words with and without Adjacent Consonants	slime, crime, stone	Spelling Rules for Split Vowel Spelling Words

Pairing Lessons with Decodable Texts

Decodable texts are most productive when learned phonics patterns align closely with the words in a text (Lindsey, 2022). Furthermore, when pupils are able to reliably apply decoding skills, they rely less on compensatory reading strategies (e.g. context clues, pictures). These strategies are commonly used by weak readers who lack strong word recognition skills (Stanovich et al, 1986; Tunmer & Chapman, 2012). Structured Literacy intervention is more effective when pupils are able to apply word reading skills directly to texts (Spear-Swerling, 2024).

Recommendations for Structure and Duration of Intervention

Recent meta-analyses of supplemental interventions found that pupils who are placed in small groups of similarly skilled pupils and receive 20–40 minutes at least three times a week make the most effective progress (Gersten et al, 2008). The flexibility of the Game Plans allow various schedules and intervention formats. Suggested practice schedules accompany each chapter to maximise skill consolidation and efficient learning. Just as an athlete develops skills in a sequential manner, the chapters in this book enhance young readers' skill development by initially teaching skills, then offering practice through drills to develop mastery, automaticity and stamina. The application to text allows readers to generalise their skills in the way that players exhibit their talents in competition.

Text Types and Purposes

Decodable texts are characterised by the level of control exerted on the variety of phonics patterns, irregular words and specialised vocabulary in the book. Texts are considered decodable when at least 64 per cent of the words can be sounded out using phonics rules (but this can extend to 95 per cent) (Reading Rockets, 2024). Strong decodable texts serve as a platform for practising word recognition and demonstrating literacy integrity (e.g. comprehensible and engaging) (Anderson et al, 1985).

Authentic texts in early literacy instruction are created for real-world purposes rather than for teaching a specific word recognition skill (Duke et al, 2006). These texts are typically rich in natural language patterns that are a mix of decodable and non-decodable words. Authentic texts may be organised by Lexile or age group.

Scan to access additional resources

Chapter 1

Beginning Decoding

- Utilising continuous blending to jump-start initial VC and CVC word reading
- Introducing a multisensory approach to spelling instruction for VC and CVC words

Game Plan

Decodable Text: ***I am Sam*, Dandelion Launchers Units 1-3, Book 1b**
Phonics Concept: **Continuous blending of one-syllable two- and three-letter short vowel words (VC and CVC)**

Phonemic Awareness

it	sit	Tim
sat	Sam	Tam

Phonics Concept

Provide direct instruction in the phonics concept, utilising words pulled from the Reader and/or that fit the patterns you are teaching.

Letter/Sound Review

s	a	t	i	m

Single Word Reading

it	sit	Tim	sat

Sentence Reading

"I am Tim."

It is Tam.

Tam sat.

Vocabulary

Which word finishes this sentence: I don't like ___? (it)	Which word refers to a character in the story? (Tim)	Which word is an action that occurred in the past? (sat)	Which word is the opposite of stand? (sit)

Story and Comprehension Questions

Who are the characters in the story?	What does Sam tell Tim to do?	Who is the last friend to sit?

Dictation

Say (repeat word)	sit			sat		
Move (segment word)						
Spell (letter tiles)	s	i	t	s	a	t
Write (write word)	s	i	t	s	a	t

Target Skills for Game Plan

Early in reading development, pupils move through two phases of word recognition. These phases are critical to later reading fluency and comprehension.

During the Partial Alphabetic/Letters and Sounds Phase, pupils develop their understanding of the alphabetic principle – that sounds in English are represented by a letter or letters. Once letter-sound knowledge has been introduced, pupils move to the next phase of word recognition – decoding.

The Full Alphabetic/Decoding Phase of word recognition is characterised by movement from isolated letter-sound knowledge to blending letter sounds and pronouncing whole words. Instruction in this phase supports the development of pupils' ability to blend sounds in the correct sequence, starting with simple, two- and three-letter short vowel words (e.g. in, bat, hop). The Game Plan for this chapter has been developed to provide a framework for teachers to refer to when moving pupils into the Decoding Phase of reading. Along these lines, the activities and instruction provided in the Game Plan are designed to develop the following two skills in pupils who are just beginning to read:

- Decoding one-syllable two- and three-letter short vowel words (VC and CVC)
- Spelling one-syllable two- and three-letter short vowel words (VC and CVC)

Your Team

Pupils are ready for this Game Plan when they demonstrate knowledge of several consonants and at least one vowel sound. In order to jump-start decoding instruction, teachers can prioritise teaching their pupils strategies for blending as soon as a handful of consonant sounds and one short vowel sound have been introduced.

It is unnecessary to instruct pupils in all grapheme-phoneme correspondences before this critical skill can begin. Consider the requirements to blend simple VC and CVC words such as "at", "sat", "pat" and "sap". In order to accurately decode these words, pupils only need to know the grapheme-phoneme correspondences for the four letters, 's', 'a', 't' and 'p'. Educators should refer to their phonics curriculum to identify at what point such instruction in this phase of word reading can begin.

Jump-Start Guide to Decoding

Scope Sample		
Letters Taught	**Sounds**	**Words to Blend**
s, a, t, i, m	at am it	at, mat, sat am, Tam, Sam it, sit
n, o, p	ap at in ip it ot op	In addition to the words above: nap, tap, sap, map Nat, pat in, pin, tin nip, sip, tip, pip pit, sit tot, not, pot top, mop, pop
Scope Sample 2		
Letters Taught	**Sounds**	**Words to Blend**
t, b, f, n, m, i, u	it ib if in im ut ub un	bit, fit bib, fib if tin, bin, fin Tim but, nut tub bun, fun, nun

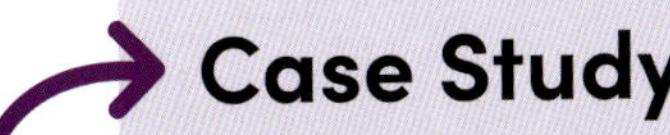

Case Study

Cameron is a Reception pupil who knows the names of the letters in her name. She is working to develop both accuracy and automaticity with additional grapheme-phoneme (sound-symbol) correspondences. During phonemic awareness and phonics instruction, her teacher notices her difficulty blending sounds into words. For example, when she attempts to blend /s/ /i/ /t/, she might say "tis". During small group instruction, her teacher reports that she identifies each sound in the word, but when attempting to pronounce the word as a unit, she is often inaccurate. What strategies can help Cameron become more accurate in both reading and spelling?

Training Camp

Before pupils are ready to blend sounds into words, they need to be accurate with a handful of consonants and at least one vowel. The following Training Camp exercises can lead to greater success in developing subsequent reading skills. These exercises incorporate multisensory techniques by including articulation cues during pronunciation to differentiate sounds of letters, as well as the use of letter formation strategies to consolidate knowledge of grapheme-phoneme correspondence.

Articulation

All letter sounds are produced through combined use of the lips, tongue, teeth, breath and soft palate. These movements, along with the vibration of the vocal cords, or lack thereof, work in a unique way to produce the nuanced sounds in the English language. In order to read, pupils must connect letters to their articulated sounds.

The /b/ sound is produced by closing the lips in a tight straight line, then building up pressure and quickly releasing in a lip-popping movement. Some programmes refer to this letter as a lip-popper or stop consonant. There are two lip-popper sounds in English – one that is voiced (/b/), and one that is unvoiced (/p/).

Voiced sounds are those that are produced by vibrating vocal cords (for example, the sounds /m/, /r/ and /v/). Unvoiced sounds are produced without making a vocal cord vibration (for example, the sounds /s/, /t/, /f/). Grouping consonant letters by their voiced and unvoiced pairs is an efficient way to cluster sounds for pupils and support the activation of multisensory cues during articulation.

Letter Formation

To help pupils associate the articulation of a letter's sound with the visual formation of the letter, educators can connect letter-sound instruction with handwriting. Handwriting involves motor planning and sequencing skills, similar to the skills required for the clear articulation of letter sounds. Research suggests that pairing formation practice with three utterances – naming the letter (if/when appropriate), naming the keyword/phrase and naming the sound – can help to solidify this knowledge in the visual word form area of the brain (McCandliss et al, 2003). In practice, pupils might name these elements as they produce the three strokes that form the letter. For the letter 'd', pupils write the half-circle belly of the letter while saying the letter name "d". As they draw the straight line up to the top, they would say the keyword ("dog", for example). Finally, as they complete the tail, they say /d/. For letters with only one or two letter strokes, prompt pupils to begin their utterances as they put pencil to paper. The connection between the three utterances and strokes can support pupils in solidifying their letter-sound knowledge. This language may be adjusted to how your particular scheme introduces and teaches letter formation.

Your Equipment

Series: Dandelion Launchers Units 1-3 (ISBN 9781907170720)

Reader: *I am Sam* (Book 1b)

Phonics Concept:

Continuous blending of one-syllable two- and three-letter short vowel words (VC and CVC).

Book Overview:

Two friends play in a park and hijinks ensue on the seesaw.

Text from the Book *I am Sam*

"I am Sam."

"I am Tim."

"Sit, Tim."

It is Tam.

Tam sat.

"Tim!"

Additional Texts

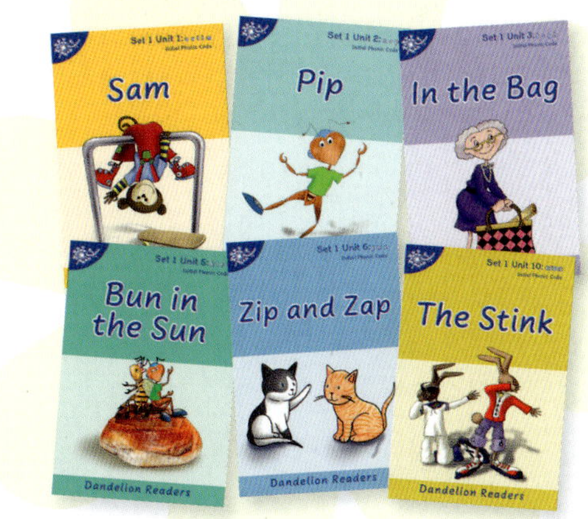

The **Dandelion Readers Sets 1-4 Units 1-10** (ISBN 9781907170027, 9781907170034, 9781907170041, 9780241687734) and **Dandelion World Stages 1-7** (ISBN 9780241666333) series follow the same phonics progression as the **Dandelion Launchers Units 1-3**, thereby providing the opportunity for instruction and application in additional texts before moving on to the next set of grapheme-phoneme correspondences.

Planning for Game Day

Game Plans are designed to provide a framework for the application of targeted phonics skills. In order to fully align practice of skills with application to connected text, a backwards planning approach is recommended. First, select the instructional focus area and a decodable text that will help reinforce the development of the targeted skills. From there, identify three sentences containing words with the target skill. These words will be used for phonemic awareness instruction, single word reading, dictation and vocabulary. For the Letter/Sound Review, identify sounds that pupils need to blend together for single word reading. Finally, set a purpose for reading and craft a variety of questions that support reading comprehension. The sequence for backwards planning is shared in the following breakout box on page 22.

Backwards Planning Using a Decodable Text

Planning Reading Activities (Sentences, Single Words and Letter Sounds)

Step 1: Choose three sentences from the text. Select sentences that offer practice for target phonics skills.

Step 2: Select four individual words that appear in the sentences for single word reading practice.

Step 3: Choose the letters and rime patterns from the single word practice to teach sound-symbol correspondence.

Planning Phonemic Awareness Activity

Use the words from the Single Word Reading activity for phonemic awareness (blending).

Planning Dictation Activity

Choose two words for the Move It, Spell It, Write It activity.

Planning Vocabulary and Comprehension Activities

Step 1: Develop questions that inquire about the meanings of the single words previously practised.

Step 2: Read the text and craft questions that require pupils to find the information in the text (factual questions) and set a purpose for reading by asking pupils to keep a particular question in mind while reading the book.

Winning Strategies

The instructional routines in the Game Plan support the ongoing development of pupils' word recognition skills through two Winning Strategies:

- Utilising continuous blending to jump-start initial VC and CVC word reading
- Introducing a multisensory approach to spelling instruction for VC and CVC words

Utilising Continuous Blending to Jump-Start Reading

Continuous blending is an evidence-based instructional strategy that enhances decoding accuracy in the early phases of reading development. Continuous blending is an alternative method to segmenting and recoding sounds. Phonics instruction that introduces decoding using a sound-by-sound blending approach focuses on retrieval of individual letter sounds, followed by the integration of sounds to produce a word. For example, to decode the word "mat", pupils are taught to point or tap under the letter 'm' and say /m/, point to the letter 'a' and say /a/, point to the last letter and say /t/ and then blend the sounds to pronounce the word "mat". There are many children who struggle with the segmentation approach to decoding and have a tendency to blend the sounds incorrectly or add additional sounds. For those pupils, the challenge lies in their ability to hold the individual sounds in the correct order, which facilitates accurate decoding. In contrast, when instruction features continuous blending, pupils are taught to sound out the word without pausing between sounds. Research that compared continuous blending with segmented blending found that pupils who received brief instruction on continuous blending demonstrated increased accuracy when decoding nonsense words (Gonzalez-Frey & Ehri, 2021). This strategy is explored in greater detail in Step 2 (page 25).

Introducing a Multisensory Approach to Spelling Instruction

Pupils' phonemic awareness skills, their decoding ability and their spelling knowledge each make an important independent contribution to word reading achievement. However, achievement is maximised when pupils are able to integrate their knowledge of the sound structure of language, grapheme-phoneme correspondences and rules for spelling (Moats & Brady, 2000). In the Move It, Spell It, Write It activity (see pages 33–34 for more about this activity), pupils segment the target word into its sounds, match the sounds to the associated letter tile and then write (spell) the word. The activity integrates development in key foundational areas. In this way, phonemic awareness, decoding and encoding are able to reinforce spelling achievement and overall literacy growth.

Executing Your Game Plan

Step 1: Maximise Phonemic Awareness Instruction

Phonemic awareness is the ability to recognise, identify and manipulate individual sounds, or phonemes, in spoken words. In order to engage in phonemic awareness activities, pupils must develop their auditory memory to distinguish between increasingly complex sequences of sounds. For example, in pre-school, most pupils can only correctly sequence large units of orally presented sounds (e.g. bath-tub, pop-corn). However, by primary school, a combination of explicit instruction and purposeful practice expands pupils' abilities to sequence individual units of sound (e.g. /s/, /u/, /n/). These skills build pupils' auditory memory, which serves as an important cognitive tool during decoding. As children decode, they must hold individual letter sounds in their auditory memory to accurately read a word. For some pupils, sequencing challenges begin at the auditory level and phonemic awareness instruction will target development of their auditory memory (National Reading Panel (US), 2000). The words chosen for the Game Plan include the targeted phonics skill. Some words are selected because pupils will read them in later activities. Other words support generalisation of phonemic awareness abilities.

Words for Phonemic Awareness Blending Activity in Game Plan

Sounds to Blend	Whole Word
/i/ /t/	it
/s/ /i/ /t/	sit
/t/ /i/ /m/	Tim
/s/ /a/ /t/	sat
/s/ /a/ /m/	Sam
/t/ /a/ /m/	Tam

Sound-Blending Routines

The phonemic awareness activity that precedes reading is always a blending activity because this offers appropriate practice for sequencing sounds in auditory memory. Critics of phonemic awareness cite the limitations of instruction in the sounds of language without connection to letters and text (Rehfeld et al, 2022). Therefore, educators should be cognisant of the pacing of instruction to ensure phonemic awareness activities do not exceed a few minutes. As pupils make errors, quick corrective feedback is recommended. Corrective feedback offers the accurate response and encourages pupils to reproduce the correct response in a "my turn" (teacher produces accurate response), "our turn" (teacher and pupils respond) and "your turn" (pupils produce accurate response) format.

Teacher Script for Introducing, Modelling and Practising Phonemic Awareness

Introduction to Strategy

Teacher: *We are going to play a mystery word game. I am going to give you the sounds, and you are going to blend them together to say the word.*

Type of Words

Choose words from the Single Word Reading section of the Game Plan or additional words that follow the same phonics concept.

Teacher Language and Prompt for Modelling

Teacher: *Watch me hold up a finger for each sound. When I connect my fingers, you will blend the sounds to say the mystery word.*

Hold up a finger as you say each sound.

Start with your left thumb if facing pupils.

Teacher: /i/ /t/

Connect your two fingers together.

Teacher: *"it".*

Differentiating Instruction or Corrective Feedback

Pupils might incorrectly pronounce the word.

Teacher: *My turn.* (Repeat the sounds in the word, hold up a finger for each sound and correctly pronounce the word.)

Teacher: *Your turn.* (Have the pupils hold up a finger while saying each sound in the word and, when they connect their fingers, pronounce the word correctly.)

Differentiation of Phonemic Awareness Instruction

Phonemic awareness is most effective when pupils are familiar with the meaning of the target word. If pupils are unfamiliar with the target word, it is recommended that educators offer an image of the word. For example, a picture of a character in a box (e.g. Tam) or less common vocabulary (e.g. picnic, cloth) could populate or be revealed once pupils have blended the sounds together.

Step 2: Teach Phonics Concepts Using Winning Strategy

The target skill for the first Game Plan is decoding VC and CVC words. To support pupils in developing decoding skills, the lesson incorporates continuous blending as a Winning Strategy. Model the continuous blending strategy with words the pupils will encounter during the Single Word Reading activity. Other words with the same target phonics skill may be incorporated for additional practice.

WINNING STRATEGY: Continuous Blending

In continuous blending, or connected phonation, pupils are explicitly taught to sound out the word without stopping or pausing between sounds. When first modelling continuous blending, choose CVC words that begin with a continuous consonant sound (e.g. f, l, m, n, f, s, v and z). These consonant sounds can be stretched out as far as your breath can sustain. Continuous sounds are easily connected to vowel sounds. It should be noted that all vowels are continuous as well. Therefore, using continuous blending for the word "mat" would sound like /mmmaaaaat/.

Teacher Script for Teaching Continuous Blending

Introduction to Strategy

Teacher: *We are going to practise a strategy today called continuous blending. When we continuously blend, we turn our voices on to blend through the entire word without turning our voices off.*

Type of Words

Two- or Three-Letter Closed Syllable Short Vowel Words (VC or CVC Words)

Teacher Language and Prompt for Modelling

Write "it" on the board.

Teacher: *Watch me. I will sweep my finger underneath each letter while saying the sound for that letter. I will hold the sound, or keep my voice on, and then glide into the sound for the next letter until I get to the last letter. This helps me blend all the sounds together without stopping. Then, I will repeat the word in a clear and crisp way.*

Sweep your finger underneath the word "it".

Teacher: */iiiiiiiit/. "it". Let's try it together. As I sweep my finger under the letters, you say and hold the sounds. I will quickly underline the word and you will repeat the word.*

For the word "sit", point to the letter 's'. Pupils should say /sssss/, holding the sound until your finger moves to the letter 'i'. They will add /i/ to /sssss/ so it sounds like /sssiii/. As you sweep your finger under the 't', pupils will add /t/ to /sssiii/ and say /sssiiit/ – "sit".

Repeat for all single words and any additional applicable practice.

Teacher: *Now let's practise with a few more.*

Supporting Pupils Having Difficulty with Continuous Blending

When selecting words for continuous blending practice, educators can choose between words that begin with continuous consonants or stop consonants.

Consonants with Continuous Sounds
f, l, m, n, r, s, v, z

Consonants with Stop Sounds
b, c (hard c), d, g, k, p, t

Pupils who struggle with continuous blending need practice with words that begin with continuous consonants (e.g. sat, mat, sit). Continuous consonants allow the sound to be held for several seconds. Stop consonants are sounds that are made quickly because they are articulated by stopping air flow. Stop sounds are best reserved for the end of words if pupils are struggling to blend. If there is a stop sound at the beginning of a word, it is often best to quickly jump off the stop consonant and link it to the vowel (e.g. /tttttim/ – "Tim").

Step 3: Reinforce Letters/Sounds in Isolation

In order to help pupils build accuracy and automaticity in matching a letter or letters to the corresponding sound(s), the Game Plan includes opportunities to practise identifying letters and sounds that appear in the text in isolation before reading them in words. The lesson features five individual letters ('s', 'a', 't', 'i', 'm'). See the **Teacher Script for Introducing, Modelling and Practising Letter/Sound Review** on page 28 for a demonstration of how to integrate this activity into a lesson. Teachers may choose to forgo the step where pupils identify the letter name if this is not consistent with the scheme.

Letter/Sound Review for Game Plan

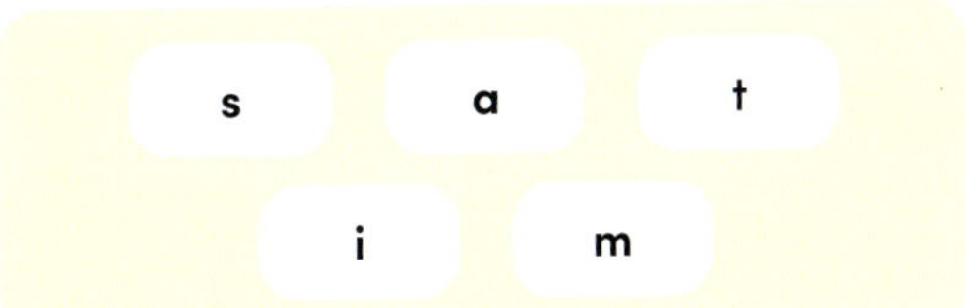

Supporting Pupils Having Difficulty with Grapheme-Phoneme Correspondence

Letter sounds are most efficiently taught when pupils accurately demonstrate basic articulation and phonemic awareness skills. For pupils who are having difficulty, consider these modifications:

- Present consonant sounds with a "clipped" pronunciation and avoid the addition of a schwa, which can confuse pupils. For example, the clipped pronunciation of the letter 'b' is /b/, as opposed to /buh/, which adds a schwa.
- Provide additional opportunities for phonemic awareness instruction, where pupils practise breaking apart the sounds in language.
- Teach articulation cues for letter sounds by helping pupils feel the placement of their lips, teeth and tongue.
- Integrate grapheme-phoneme and handwriting instruction so that pupils are able to recognise the letter, pair the letter with the corresponding sound and form the letter appropriately.

Teacher Script for Introducing, Modelling, and Practising Letter/Sound Review

Introduction to Strategy

Teacher: *We are going to review some letters and sounds to help us with our reading.*

Type of Words

Choose individual consonants and vowels from the Game Plan.

Teacher Language and Prompt for Modelling

Write the first letter to review on a whiteboard or utilise letter-sound cards from your curriculum resources.

Teacher: *The letter is ___.* (Point to the letter and say the letter name if appropriate.)

Pupils repeat.

Teacher: *The sound is ____.* (Point to the letter and say the sound.)

Pupils repeat.

Continue with each letter or pattern to complete the routine.

If using letter-sound cards from a different curriculum, include the keyword or image as necessary. Note that the keyword is used to support pupils in the appropriate production of the sound. It is important to fade this scaffold once pupils are able to accurately produce the sound.

Maintaining a "Perky Pace"

In order to keep the lesson moving at a "perky pace", it is important to establish a routine that maximises pupils' engagement with the material. In the book *Explicit Instruction: Effective and Efficient Teaching*, Archer and Hughes emphasise the importance of whole group participation (Archer & Hughes, 2011). They recommend teaching pupils a signal (verbal and/or nonverbal) that cues choral responses. Just as a chorus includes the voices of all participants, choral responses invite all pupils to answer simultaneously. For example, you might tap your finger under the letter(s) and teach pupils to respond with the sound, or you might tap and say "sound" to elicit a quick, choral response from all pupils. Choral responses are a powerful interactive tool when there is one brief, correct answer. If pupils answer incorrectly, teachers can prompt corrective feedback in a "my turn, your turn" manner. Archer and Hughes recommend refraining from relying on individual turn-taking or hand-raising during these periods of instruction because doing so reduces opportunities for engagement and hampers the pace of instruction. When there is more than one correct answer, teachers can utilise a turn-and-talk method, in which pupils are paired and take it in turns to share their ideas. (See Chapter 2 (page 56) for more about the turn-and-talk method.)

Step 4: Apply Phonics Concept to Single Words from the Text

The lesson's single words achieve three goals: they are in the story, they are in the sentences you have selected and they provide the opportunity for pupils to practise the target phonics skill(s). The Game Plan features four words from the story *I am Sam* (e.g. it, sit, Tim, sat). See the **Teacher Script for Continuous Blending** on page 26 to practise continuous blending with single words from the text.

Individual Words for Game Plan

it	sit	Tim	sat

Step 5: Practise Reading Sentences from the Text

The sentence reading routine provides pupils with an opportunity to apply their decoding skills to connected text. Ideal sentences contain words with the target phonics concept and are comprehensible as standalone sentences. In some cases, it may be necessary to modify the sentence slightly to replace a pronoun with the name of the character. Pupils read these sentences prior to reading the decodable text, so it can be helpful to choose sentences that highlight characters' names and allude to important components or events in the text. For the Game Plan, we have selected the following sentences from *I am Sam* because they include a variety of VC and CVC words and introduce two of the characters in the story.

Sentences for Game Plan

"I am Tim."

It is Tam.

Tam sat.

Step 6: Expand Text-Related Vocabulary Knowledge

A key feature that distinguishes Structured Literacy instruction from solitary phonics instruction is the integration of various aspects of word knowledge. Vocabulary is a critical aspect of word knowledge, as it supports both reading fluency and comprehension. As pupils build beginning decoding skills, connections between word recognition abilities and comprehension occur partially through vocabulary instruction. In fact, a prominent theory of reading comprehension developed by Philip Gough and William Tunmer, called the Simple View of Reading, suggests that reading comprehension is the product of decoding skills and language comprehension skills, including vocabulary knowledge (Gough & Tunmer, 1986).

Evidence indicates that pupils recognise words not only because of their knowledge of letters and their corresponding sounds but also because of their knowledge of the word's meaning. Strong vocabulary knowledge allows readers to access a mental lexicon, a mental dictionary of words, which aids in fluent reading by helping them recognise and interpret words effortlessly (Perfetti, 2007). As readers grow their vocabulary, they develop a better understanding of these linguistic features, which makes it easier to recognise words even in varied contexts (Ehri, 2005). This connection is particularly crucial for young readers as they acquire foundational reading skills and become capable of reading fluently (National Reading Panel (US), 2000).

The Game Plan features a simple vocabulary activity where teachers review meanings for previously practised individual words. Questions can incorporate references to synonyms, antonyms and characters in the story, or they may offer pupils opportunities to complete a sentence. Prior to the activity, display the words from the Single Word Reading portion of the Game Plan. Have pupils chorally read the list before beginning to ask the questions.

Support Language Comprehension Among Multilingual Learners

For pupils who are learning English as a new language, it might be helpful to provide images along with each of the single words for this activity. Linking the sounds, spelling and meaning will help support pupils in developing both their word recognition and language comprehension skills.

Words and Questions for Vocabulary Activity

Game Plan: *I am Sam*	**Questions**
sat	Which word is an action that occurred in the past?
Tim	Which word refers to a character in the story?
it	Which word finishes this sentence? I don't like_____.
sit	Which word is the opposite of stand?

Game Plan: *On the Mat*	**Questions**
mat	Which word means a small rug?
sat	Which word completes the blank in this sentence? When I got home, I _____ down to eat.
Tim	Which word or words refer to a character in the story?
sit	Fill in the blank in this sentence. Before I give my dog a treat, I tell him to _____.

Step 7: Putting It All Together for Text Reading and Comprehension

The book reading portion of the Game Plan offers pupils the opportunity to apply their single word and sentence reading skills in connected text. Practising connected text reading is a critical tool in improving accuracy, fluency and comprehension (National Reading Panel (US), 2000). During this activity, including a series of comprehension questions that connect word reading with meaning is recommended. When crafting questions to go with the decodable book, ensure that the questions can be answered by reading the text, not by referencing the pictures. Typical questions can include a range of question types. These may include literal, inferential and evaluative questions, as well as questions based on vocabulary knowledge. Prior to asking pupils to read connected text, teachers can orient pupils to the book by previewing the title and illustrations. Furthermore, setting a purpose for pupils to aim for when reading supports active comprehension monitoring (e.g. "As we read, I want you to work out the problem that our main character encounters in the book."). Note that in some programmes, comprehension activities may only occur with text read to the pupil. However, in a multi-componential approach, comprehension questions can be utilised with text pupils have read themselves.

Comprehension Questions for Game Plan

Factual
What are the characters in the story?

Factual
What does Sam tell Tim to do?

Inferential
Who is the last friend to sit?

Text from the Book *I am Sam*

"I am Sam."

"I am Tim."

"Sit, Tim."

It is Tam.

Tam sat.

"Tim!"

Use Choral or Partner Reading Instead of Round Robin

Strong engagement activities maximise participation and ensure that all pupils receive adequate time to build their reading skills. The three primary engagement techniques are choral reading, partner reading and whisper reading to oneself. These techniques are often interchangeable. Some educators might have all pupils chorally read the first two pages and then pair off to partner read the rest of the story. Other teachers might opt for some pupils to partner read or read to themselves. Teachers may choose to use the technique of "tapping in" where pupils are independently reading aloud. The teacher pauses to listen to individual pupils and taps each pupil for a turn to read aloud. The "oral" part can be accomplished at full volume or at a whisper; the key feature is that the pupil articulates the words and receives auditory feedback by hearing their voice. Whisper phones are particularly helpful for this purpose. The strategy that should be actively avoided or used with minimal frequency is the "round robin" approach, where each pupil in a group takes a turn reading a line of text while the others follow along. When pupils are only responsible for a minimal portion of the text, it restricts skill building and limits their opportunities to build stamina (Kuhn, 2014).

Step 8: Applying Phonics Knowledge to Dictation

The reciprocal connection between reading and spelling in literacy achievement has been well established in literature (Moats & Brady, 2000). Both reading and spelling rely on pupils' knowledge of sounds and corresponding letters. Spelling is often more challenging for pupils because, although English has a limited number of sounds (approximately 44 sounds/phonemes, depending on region and curricular tool), there are many different letter patterns, or graphemes, for spelling each sound. For example, the /ae/ sound (also depicted as /ai/, /ā/ or /A/) can be spelt 'a', 'a-e', 'ay', 'ai', 'ea', 'eigh' and 'ey'. Most pupils require a comprehensive approach to spelling that simultaneously integrates their knowledge of all contributing skills, including the sounds in language (phonemic awareness), the letter patterns and correct sequencing of each sound (phonics).

This Game Plan features a multisensory instructional strategy called Move It, Spell It, Write It that supports the integration of phonemic awareness, phonics skills and letter formation skills as pupils spell words (Blachman et al, 2000). Later chapters fade these scaffolds in order to expand pupils' spelling from sounds and individual words to complex sentence writing. If at any time your pupils struggle with spelling, scaffolds from Move It, Spell It, Write It can be re-integrated into the lesson to support skill development.

WINNING STRATEGY: Introducing a Multisensory Approach to Spelling Instruction

Move It, Spell It, Write It is a multisensory spelling activity. This activity combines phonemic awareness, grapheme-phoneme correspondence and handwriting to practise the targeted phonics concept. It is a modified version of a widely used activity called Say-It-and-Write-It (Blachman et al, 2000). An Elkonin Spelling Mat is used for this activity.

Elkonin Boxes

Elkonin boxes, also called phoneme frames or sound boxes, are tools that can be used as part of a method of teaching that aids in the development of phonemic awareness skills. Pupils can practise the Move It, Spell It, Write It activity with these boxes. To use Elkonin boxes, teachers draw a series of boxes on paper or a whiteboard, with one box representing each sound in the target word. Pupils listen and repeat the target word, then move a token into each box for each phoneme in the word. For example, for the word "sat", the teacher would draw three boxes, one box for each of the sounds in "sat".

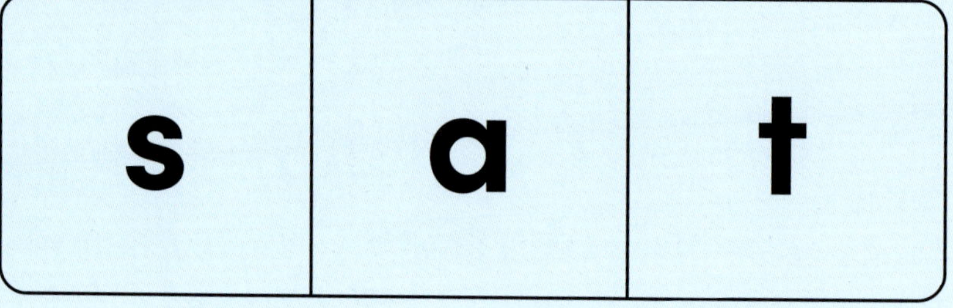

During the "Move It" portion of the activity, teachers provide pupils with an Elkonin Spelling Mat, present the word and guide pupils in dividing the word into individual sound segments. Each sound is initially represented with a token, which pupils move into the appropriate Elkonin box. For some pupils, the initial target skill may involve simply completing the "Move It" portion of the exercise. Others are ready to progress to "Spell It".

During "Spell It", teachers guide pupils in identifying the letters that represent each sound in the Elkonin boxes. Then, they instruct them to place the appropriate letter tile or magnetic letter under the sound. Finally, in the "Write It" portion of the task, pupils write the letters to spell the target word. The Game Plan features two words – "sit" and "sat" – that follow the phonics concept and are featured in the Move It, Spell It, Write It activity. Depending on the progression of your phonics programme, the point at which this skill is introduced may vary. Some programmes may not utilise spelling activities such as this one until pupils are introduced to more complex words.

Teacher Script for Delivering the Move It, Spell It, Write It Activity

Introduction to Strategy

Give pupils a Move It, Spell It, Write It paper, the appropriate number of tokens needed to represent each sound in the word and letter tiles/magnetic letters that correspond to the letters in the target word in the Game Plan. Do not put the letters out in the correct sequence.

Teacher: *We are going to connect a word we have been reading to our spelling work.*

Teacher Language and Prompt for Move It

Teacher: *Today our word to spell is ______. Say ______.*

Pupils repeat the word.

Teacher: *_____ has _____ sounds. Let's say each sound and move the tokens into the boxes below. Move one token for each sound you say.*

Pupils segment the word while simultaneously moving one token for each sound into an Elkonin box.

Teacher: *Say the word _____.*

Pupils complete the request.

Teacher Language and Prompt for Spell It

Teacher: *Now that we have identified the sounds in our word, let's use our letters to spell the sounds.*

Point to the first token in the Elkonin box, elicit the first sound and have pupils match the sound with the correct letter tile/ magnetic letter. Repeat for each token.

Teacher: *The sound ____ is spelt with the letter ____.* (Elicit the letter name.)

Repeat with each token until the word has been spelt with the letter tiles/magnetic letters.

Teacher Language and Prompt for Write It

If a specific handwriting or dictation paper is used in your phonics programme, consider using it for this portion of the activity.

Teacher: *Now that we have spelt our word, let's write it. The word is ____.*

Pupils repeat the word.

Teacher: *The first sound in the word is ____. What letter do we write here?*

Pupils respond.

Teacher: *Write the letter ____.*

Model the letter formation on a whiteboard or paper, using language consistent with your handwriting instruction.

Repeat the procedure with each letter until pupils have written the word.

Teacher: *Let's read the word together.*

Pupils run a finger under the word while reading it.

Proposed Practice Schedule

The Game Plan in this chapter represents a set of eight instructional routines for small group instruction designed to be delivered over the course of several sessions in addition to your whole group phonics scheme. Research suggests that deliberate and spaced practice is effective for adopting new skills (Archer & Hughes, 2011). Although the practice schedule can be adjusted to align with your allotted instructional time, ensuring that there is dedicated time for connected text practice each day should be prioritised.

Day 1 (15 mins)	**Day 2 (15 mins)**
Phonemic Awareness (2 mins)	Vocabulary (3 mins)
Phonics Concept (4 mins)	Book Reading (5 mins)
Letter/Sound Review (2 mins)	Comprehension Questions (2 mins)
Single Words (2 mins)	Dictation (5 mins)
Sentences (5 mins)	

Game Plan

Decodable Text: ***On the Mat*, Dandelion Launchers Units 1-3, Book 1d**
Phonics Concept: **Continuous blending of one-syllable two- and three-letter short vowel words (VC and CVC)**

Phonemic Awareness

on	sit	mat
am	Sam	Tam

Phonics Concept

Provide direct instruction in the phonics concept, utilising words pulled from the Reader and/or that fit the patterns you are teaching.

Letter/Sound Review

s	a	t	i	m

Single Word Reading

Sam	mat	sit	Tim

Sentence Reading

Sam is on the mat.

Tam is on Sam.

"Tim, sit on Tam."

Vocabulary

Which word means a small rug? (mat)	Which word completes the blank in this sentence? I sat ____ the floor. (on)	Which word refers to a character in the story? (Tim/Tam/Sam)	Fill in the blank in this sentence. Before I give my dog a treat, I tell him to ___. (sit)

Story and Comprehension Questions

Who are the characters in the story?	What did Tam do?	Who sat first? Who sat last?

Dictation

Say (repeat word)	mat			Sam		
Move (segment word)	●	●	●	●	●	●
Spell (letter tiles)	m	a	t	s	a	m
Write (write word)	m	a	t	S	a	m

Chapter 2

Developing Automaticity with Simple Decoding

- Recognising rime patterns in words
- Backwards decoding
- Strategic instruction for heart words
- Reinforcing word recognition through spelling

Game Plan

Decodable Text: ***Sit, Sam,* Dandelion Readers Set 3 Units 1-10, Book 1**
Phonics Concept: **Rime pattern recognition of two- and three-letter short vowel words (VC and CVC)**

Phonemic Awareness			Phonics Concept
it	sit	Sam	Provide direct instruction in the phonics concept, utilising words pulled from the Reader and/or that fit the patterns you are teaching.
mat	sat	Tam	

Letter/Sound/Rime Review

s-	t-	m-	-am	-it	-at

Single Word Reading

sit	sat	Sam	Tam

Heart Words

the

Sentence Reading

Sam sat on the mat.

"Sam, sit on it."

Tam sat on the mat.

Vocabulary

Which words are names? (Sam/Tam)	Which word completes the blank in this sentence? I am tired and need to find a chair to ____ in? (sit)	Which word is the opposite of stand? (sit)	Which word completes the blank in this sentence? Yesterday, at the football game, we ____ in the stands. (sat)

Story and Comprehension Questions

Who sat on the mat first?	Who sat on the mat last?	Why did Tam ask Sam to sit on the mat?

Dictation

Heart Word	the
Letters/Sounds/Rime Patterns	-at, -it, -am
Words	sat, sit, Sam
Sentence	Sam sat on the mat.

Target Skills for Game Plan

As pupils move from the Full Alphabetic/ Decoding Phase of word recognition to the Partial Mapping Phase, they rely less on blending each letter sound to pronounce whole words and begin to automatically recognise larger units of language. Attention to larger word parts results in greater efficiency and automaticity in reading. The activities and instruction in the Game Plan are designed to develop the following two skills:

- Automatic decoding of two- and three-letter short vowel words (VC and CVC)
- Automatic spelling of two- and three-letter short vowel words (VC and CVC)

Your Team

Pupils are ready for this Game Plan once they can accurately identify short vowels and consonant sounds in isolation. Pupils at this phase of word recognition may rely too heavily on sounding out each word, which can hinder their overall reading fluency and affect their comprehension of the text.

Case Study

Matteo, a Reception pupil, is accurate with letter sounds in isolation and, with prompting, can slowly blend sounds to form a word. Currently, he relies on the continuous blending strategy to decode words. On a measure of nonsense word fluency, he is able to meet benchmark expectations for correct letter sounds but is not yet automatic or fluent enough to meet the expectations for reading the whole word. What strategies can help Matteo become more fluent in both reading and spelling?

Your Equipment

Series: Dandelion Readers Set 3 Units 1-10
(ISBN 9781907170041)
Reader: *Sit, Sam* (Book 1)
Phonics Concept:
Rime pattern recognition of two- and three-letter short vowel words (VC and CVC).
Book Overview:
Two friends go on a wild carpet ride and learn a valuable lesson.

Text from the Book *Sit, Sam*

Tam sat on the mat.

"Sam, sit on it."

"Sit, Sam, sit."

"Sit on it, Sam."

"Tam! Tam!"

Sam sat on the mat.

Additional Texts

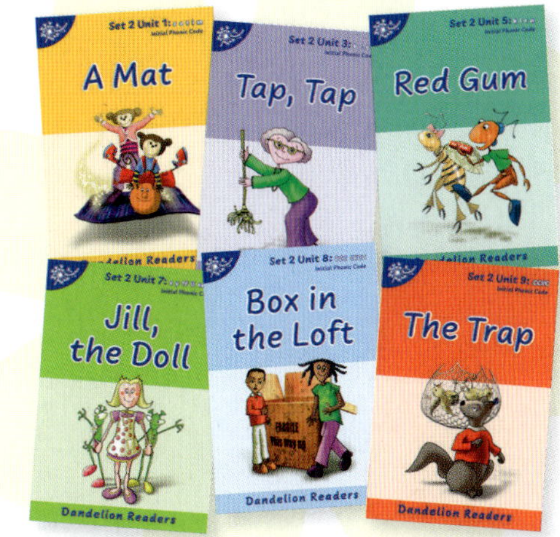

The **Dandelion Readers Set 1 Units 1-10** (ISBN 9781907170027) and **Set 2 Units 1-10** (ISBN 9781907170034) follow the same phonics progression as the **Dandelion Readers Set 3 Units 1-10**, thereby providing the opportunity for instruction and application in additional texts before moving on to the next set of grapheme-phoneme correspondences.

Planning for Game Day

The Game Plan in Chapter 2 was designed using the same backwards planning approach as Chapter 1. Backwards planning ensures the activities in the Structured Literacy routines are aligned with the patterns, vocabulary and text pupils will encounter in the accompanying book. First, select the instructional focus area and a decodable text that will help reinforce the development of the targeted skills. From there, identify three sentences containing words with the target skill. These words will be used for phonemic awareness instruction, single word reading, dictation and vocabulary. For the Letter/Sound/Rime Review, identify sounds that pupils need to blend together for single word reading. Finally, set a purpose for reading and craft a variety of questions that support reading comprehension. The sequence for backwards planning is shared in the following breakout box on page 42.

Backwards Planning Using a Decodable Text

Planning Reading Activities (Sentences, Single Words and Letter Sounds)

Step 1: Choose three sentences from the text. Select sentences that offer practice for target phonics skills.

Step 2: Select four individual words that appear in the sentences for single word reading practice.

Step 3: Choose the letters and rime patterns from the single word practice to teach sound-symbol correspondence.

Planning Phonemic Awareness Activity

Use the words from the Single Word Reading activity for phonemic awareness (blending).

Planning Heart Word and Dictation Activity

Step 1: Choose up to four heart words from the text.

Step 2: Select rime patterns, one heart word, three single words and at least one sentence from the reading activities for dictation tasks.

Planning Vocabulary and Comprehension Activities

Step 1: Develop questions that inquire about the meanings of the single words previously practised.

Step 2: Read the text and craft questions that require pupils to find the information in the text (factual questions), analyse word meaning (semantic questions) or "read between the lines" to understand the deeper purpose of the story (inference questions). Set a purpose for reading by asking pupils to keep a particular question in mind while reading the book.

Winning Strategies

The instructional routines in the Game Plan support the ongoing development of pupils' word recognition skills through four Winning Strategies:

- Recognising rime patterns in words
- Backwards decoding
- Strategic instruction for heart words
- Reinforcing word recognition through spelling

Recognising Rime Patterns in Words

One of the largest and most consistent units in English words is called the rime pattern. A rime pattern consists of the vowel and any subsequent consonants within that word/ syllable. In the word "sat", the rime pattern is "-at". The letters preceding the rime pattern are linguistically referred to as the onset, but throughout *The Structured Literacy Playbook*, the term "starter" will be used.

Instruction in rime patterns, sometimes referred to as analytic phonics, has been proven equally effective for young readers as the sound-by-sound synthetic approach (National Reading Panel (US), 2000). Rime pattern instruction is particularly helpful for developing word recognition for several reasons. First, it highlights a "chunk" of a word, as opposed to an individual letter; next, it encourages reading across the entire word (Kilpatrick, 2015); and finally, rime pattern instruction supports the correct pronunciation of the vowel. In English words, vowel sounds are controlled by the letters that follow them, not those that precede them. For example, the words below all begin with the letters 'be', but the pronunciation of the vowel sound changes in each word, and this change is governed by the letters (or lack thereof) after the vowel 'e'.

Differences in Vowel Pronunciation Based on Rime Patterns in Words

be	best	beast	berate

Backwards Decoding

Backwards decoding is an effective instructional technique that supports partial orthographic mapping. During the process of backwards decoding, pupils read the rime pattern before reading the starter sound. Although this backwards approach may seem counterintuitive at first, reading words from back to front actually capitalises on the cognitive processes used for word recognition. The ability to recognise words automatically without decoding relies on several underlying foundational skills, including a reader's auditory memory for sound sequences (Kilpatrick, 2015). Evidence indicates that humans store words in their auditory memory using two major phonological cues: the first sound and the rime pattern. Reading words by rime pattern is a practice that not only activates a pupil's auditory memory for all the words that they know with that pattern but also, as was noted earlier, supports pupils in producing the correct pronunciation of the vowel. For example, when pupils backwards decode the word "went" by reading the rime pattern "-ent" first, all of the words in their auditory memory that contain a similar or matching rime pattern are activated (e.g. bent, sent, tent, went). When the starter sound is added to the rime pattern, the pupils are more likely to accurately pronounce and map the entire word.

Strategic Instruction for Heart Words

A significant proportion of words in the English language do not follow common phonetic rules. These words can be recognised by their irregular spelling patterns (for example, the, said, have, from). Words with irregular spelling patterns occur frequently in text and are therefore a common part of early literacy instruction. The terms that educators use for these words vary by the curriculum and may include "high-frequency words", "trick words" or "red words", to name a few. In *The Structured Literacy Playbook*, these commonly occurring irregular words are called heart words, and it is recommended that pupils are taught the related letter patterns for reading and spelling using a strategic approach called Heart Word Magic. Heart Word Magic was developed by Really Great Reading to support pupils' word analysis skills. The instructional approach is helpful in the way that it emphasises using knowledge of traditional letter-sound relationships and while also noting irregular patterns (Really Great Reading, 2024). Utilising a word's sound sequence and stressing the letter or letters that produce each sound has strong research-based support (Kilpatrick, 2020); it aids in pupils' overall ability to "map" the word for rapid recognition in the future.

Reinforcing Word Recognition Through Spelling

Strategic, explicit and systematic dictation activities play a crucial role in literacy achievement. These activities go beyond mere memorisation; they focus on developing understanding of phonetic patterns, spelling rules and morphophonemic structures within language (Galuschka et al, 2020). When instruction is systematic, pupils are guided in a step-by-step manner. This process ensures that each skill builds logically upon the previous one, helping to prevent gaps in foundational knowledge. Systematic spelling practice reinforces the connections between sounds and letters, enabling pupils to decode and encode more effectively (Graham & Santangelo, 2014).

Moreover, these structured activities foster pupils' phonemic awareness, allowing them to distinguish and manipulate sounds – a core skill in reading and writing fluency. Dictation activities that are aligned with the sounds, single words and sentences from their text offer a dual benefit. They help reinforce the correct pronunciation and spelling of words in context. Over time, this cohesive approach offers reciprocal benefits to pupils: spelling skills are enhanced by reading achievement, and reading achievement strengthens spelling automaticity and accuracy.

Simultaneous Oral Spelling Strategy (SOS)

Simultaneous Oral Spelling (SOS) is a multisensory teaching procedure used to help pupils improve their spelling. By saying each sound in the word aloud and visualising each letter before writing it down, pupils connect the phonological, visual and auditory processes needed for accurate spelling. The SOS steps are below.

1. Teacher says the word for spelling.
2. Pupils repeat the word.
3. Starting with the thumb, pupils sound out the word, holding up one finger for each sound. (Pupils needing support might skip or add a sound. Use Elkonin boxes and counters or tokens to help the pupils visually represent each sound in the word.)
4. Starting with the thumb again, pupils now "finger spell" the word, holding up one finger for each letter. Make sure pupils are saying each letter out loud.
5. Pupils are now ready to write the word. Coach pupils to say each letter as they put pencil to paper.
6. Finally, pupils read the word aloud.

Executing Your Game Plan

Step 1: Maximise Phonemic Awareness Instruction

Our ability to recognise, identify and manipulate individual sounds in spoken words is called phonemic awareness. Phonemic awareness activities that have high utility include blending and segmenting. These skills are the most closely related to our abilities to decode and encode. In the Game Plan, the words used in the phonemic awareness activities are pulled directly from the text and address the lesson's target phonics skills. If the text offers a limited selection of practice words, bolster your activity with additional words that follow your target pattern. See Chapter 1 (pages 24–26) for more about blending sounds.

Words for Phonemic Awareness Blending Activity in Game Plan

Sounds to Blend	Whole Word
/i/ /t/	it
/s/ /i/ /t/	sit
/s/ /a/ /m/	Sam
/m/ /a/ /t/	mat
/s/ /a/ /t/	sat
/t/ /a/ /m/	Tam

Step 2: Teach Phonics Concepts Using Winning Strategies

The target phonics skills for the Game Plan are automatic decoding and spelling of two- and three-letter short vowel words (VC and CVC). In order to achieve these goals, the lesson incorporates two Winning Strategies that move pupils towards greater automaticity in recognising letter pattern chunks: recognising rime patterns in words and backwards decoding.

Select several CVC words to use for instruction. Consider the skill level of your pupils. Pupils with the greatest level of need will benefit from a tightly controlled lesson in which a limited number of words are used for modelling and practice. The Teacher Scripts that follow on pages 47 and 48 are designed for pupils who know the consonants 's', 'p', 'm', 't' and 'd', as well as the vowels 'a' and 'i'.

WINNING STRATEGY: Recognising Rime Patterns in Words

Rime pattern instruction is particularly helpful for developing sight word recognition for several reasons. First, it highlights a chunk of a word as opposed to an individual letter; next, it encourages reading across the entire word (Kilpatrick, 2020); and finally, rime pattern instruction supports the correct pronunciation of the vowel.

Most children are not familiar with strategies for either identifying or reading words by rime pattern. The first step for a teacher is introducing the universal presence of rime patterns in all English words. Then, work with pupils to support their independent ability to recognise the rime patterns in words. See the **Teacher Script for Recognising Rime Patterns** on page 47 and the **Teacher Script for Practising Backwards Decoding** on page 48 for a model of how to introduce this strategy in a lesson.

Teacher Script for Recognising Rime Patterns

Introduction to Strategy

Teacher: *Did you know that every word has at least one rime pattern? Rime patterns start with a vowel sound and usually end with consonant sounds. Let's practise underlining the rime pattern in a few words.*

Type of Words

Three-Letter Closed Syllable Short Vowel Words (CVC Words)

Teacher Language and Prompt for Modelling

Write "tip" on the board.

Teacher: *Let's find and underline our first rime pattern. I am going to run my finger under the letters of the first word. When I come to the letter making a vowel sound, put your hand in the air.* (Stop when your finger reaches the vowel 'i'.)

Teacher: *This letter 'i' is making the vowel sound /i/. This is where our rime pattern starts.* (Begin underline.) *The rime pattern ends with the letter 'p'.* (Conclude underline.) *The rime pattern is "-ip".* (Prompt pupils to repeat.) *Now let's practise with a few more.*

Additional Practice

sip **mat** **sad**

WINNING STRATEGY: Backwards Decoding

Once pupils understand the concept of a rime pattern and can identify the rime pattern in a three-letter short vowel word (CVC), guidance is provided on reading words by rime pattern. This strategy is called backwards decoding and increases the automaticity with which pupils recognise words.

In order to backwards decode, pupils are instructed to first read the rime pattern, then pronounce the starter sound in isolation and finally blend the sounds together to produce the entire word. During the Single Word Reading activity, apply the backwards decoding technique to the single words from the Game Plan.

Teacher Script for Practising Backwards Decoding

Introduction to Strategy

Teacher: *We have already practised identifying and underlining the rime pattern. Now our rime pattern is going to help us read words more quickly. We are going to read the rime pattern first using a technique called backwards decoding.*

Type of Words

Three-Letter Closed Syllable Short Vowel Words (CVC Words)

Teacher Language and Prompt for Modelling

Return to word list (tip, sip, mat, sad).

Teacher: *Let's look at the first word. We have already underlined the rime pattern. Now I am going to read the word starting with the rime pattern. Watch me. "-ip". When I say "rime pattern", you read the pattern.* (Elicit "-ip".) *Now I am going to read the starter sound. Watch me. "t-".*

Teacher: *When I say "starter sound", I want you to only read the starter sound.* (Elicit "t-".) *Now I am going to blend the two parts together. Watch me.* "tip". *When I say "blend", I want you to blend the starter sound and rime pattern.* (Elicit "tip".) *Now let's practise with a few more.*

Additional Practice

s<u>ad</u>: ad - s - sad

s<u>ip</u>: ip - s - sip

m<u>at</u>: at - m - mat

Step 3: Reinforce Letters/Sounds in Isolation

The Game Plan includes opportunities to practise identifying letters/rime patterns and corresponding sounds that appear in the text in isolation before reading them in words. Teaching familiar letter patterns such as rime units facilitates the recognition of word parts and enables greater automaticity in word recognition and spelling. The lesson features several different sounds to practise in isolation: three consonant starter sounds, /s/, /t/ and /m/, as well as the rime patterns "-am", "-it" and "-at". See **Letter/Sound/Rime Review for Game Plan** on page 49.

See Chapter 1 (page 28) for **Teacher Script for Introducing, Modelling and Practising Letter/Sound Review** as necessary. For guidance on practising letter sounds and rime patterns in isolation, see the following teacher scripts.

Letter/Sound/Rime Review for Game Plan

Teacher Script for Letter/Sound/Rime Review: Single Letters

Introduction to Strategy

Teacher: *We are going to review some letters and sounds to help us with our reading.*

Type of Letters

Choose individual consonants and vowels from the Game Plan.

Write the first letter to review on a whiteboard or utilise letter/sound cards from your curriculum resources.

Teacher: *The letter is ____.* (Point to the letter and say the letter name. In some programmes, knowledge of letter names may come at a later stage.)

Pupils repeat.

Teacher: *The sound to say is ____.* (Point to the letter and say the sound.)

Pupils repeat.

Continue with each letter.

If using letter/sound cards from a different curriculum, include keywords or images as needed.

Additional Practice

The Game Plan suggests reviewing six letters/letter patterns. You may choose to add additional letters for review, but keep in mind this portion of the routine should be brief.

Corrective Feedback

Since this activity is teacher-led, corrective feedback may not be necessary. To reduce the scaffolds, consider eliciting the letter name (if appropriate) and/or sound as opposed to providing it for the pupils.

Teacher: *The letter is ____.* (Point to the letter and elicit the name.)

Pupils respond.

Teacher: *The sound to say is ____.* (Point to the letter and elicit the sound.)

Pupils respond.

Teacher Script for Letter/Sound/Rime Review: Rime Patterns

Introduction to Strategy

Teacher: *We are going to review some rime patterns to help us with our reading.*

Type of Letters

Choose rime patterns from the Game Plan or additional rime patterns to review.

Write the first rime pattern to review on a whiteboard.

Teacher: *The rime pattern is ____.* (Point to the rime pattern and pronounce the rime pattern.) *What's the rime pattern?*

Pupils respond.

Teacher: *The letters are ____.* (Point to the rime pattern and name the letters.) *What are the letters?*

Pupils repeat.

Continue with each letter.

If using letter/sound cards from a different curriculum, include keywords or images as needed.

Additional Practice

The Game Plan suggests up to six letters/rime patterns. You may choose to add additional letters/rime patterns for review, but keep in mind this portion of the routine should be brief.

Corrective Feedback

Since this activity is teacher-led, corrective feedback may not be necessary. To reduce the scaffolds, consider eliciting the rime pattern as opposed to providing it for the pupils.

Teacher: *The rime pattern is ____.* (Point to the rime pattern and elicit the correct response.)

Pupils respond.

Step 4: Apply Phonics Concept to Single Words from the Text

The Game Plan features four words from the story *Sit, Sam*. These are "sit", "sat", "Sam" and "Tam". These words provide practice reading three-letter short vowel words (CVC words) and applying the Winning Strategy of backwards decoding.

Individual Words for Game Plan

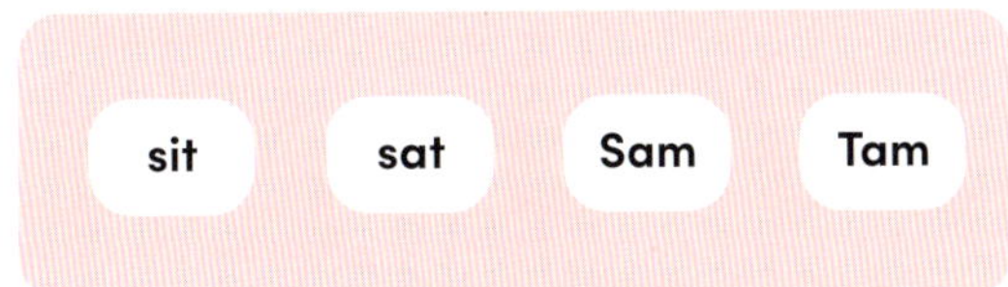

Read the Single Words Using Backwards Decoding

Now that pupils understand the concept of backwards decoding, instruct them in using the strategy with individual words from the text. Refer to the **Teacher Script for Practising Backwards Decoding** in Step 2 for guidance on coaching pupils with the backwards decoding approach. As you practise, reduce the teacher language and provide short prompts that elicit choral responses from your pupils. Reducing teacher language and increasing unison responses affords pupils multiple opportunities to practise, which maximises skill development.

Step 5: Build Knowledge of Heart Words

Most texts contain frequently occurring "tricky" words that break the rules of phonics and are challenging to decode. The Game Plans refer to these as heart words, because the tricky part must be learnt by heart. As pupils progress through phonics instruction, the list of heart words often changes. For example, before pupils learn words with split vowel (vowel-consonant-e) spelling patterns, the words "fine", "rope" and "Pete" are heart words, but only temporarily. Pupils will eventually learn the phonics rules for these words. Other heart words can be considered permanent, as they break all phonics rules. Permanent heart words include "said", "where" and "some".

Teachers can utilise their curriculum as a resource for determining which heart words are suitable for the current lesson, or they may select alternate heart words from the series recommended for this chapter. See **Selected Heart Words from Dandelion Readers Series Organised by Sound and Irregular Spelling** on page 52 to see a selection of heart words from the Reader *Pip, Sam and Tam*.

Selected Heart Words from Dandelion Readers Series Organised by Sound and Irregular Spelling

Title	Sound 1	Sound 2	Text
Pip, Sam and Tam	/i/	/z/	Tam **is** on top of Sam. Pip **is** on top of Tam. Pip **is** not on top. Tam **is** not on top.
	i	s	

Title	Sound 1	Sound 2	Text
Pip, Sam and Tam	/u/	/v/	Pip is on top **of** Tam.
	o	f	

Depending on the progression of your phonics programme, your pupils may have already been taught the phonics patterns in certain temporary heart words. If that is the case, you may choose an additional word or simply use the strategy as a spelling review and do not use the heart.

WINNING STRATEGY: Strategic Instruction for Heart Words

The heart word strategy for learning irregular words capitalises on the idea that each heart word has only one or two irregular spelling features. Rather than instructing a pupil to memorise the whole word, heart word instruction provides a strategy that emphasises segmenting the sounds in the word, producing the phonetically regular spellings for sounds and memorising the one or two irregularly spelt sounds. This Winning Strategy will help pupils in identifying these tricky words by capitalising on the aspects of the words that are familiar and drawing attention to those parts that need to be remembered by heart.

Teacher Script for Modelling and Practising Reading and Writing Heart Words

Introduction to Strategy

Teacher: *Some words we read in English do not follow the phonics patterns we have learnt. We call these words heart words, and we will use a new strategy for learning to read and spell these words. Since the words are not following the rules, we have to remember part of their spelling by heart. Let me show you how it works.*

Type of Words

Choose high-frequency words that are irregularly spelt.

Teacher: *The heart word today is _____.* (Teacher writes the word on the board and uses the word in a sentence.) *Say _______.*

Pupils repeat the word.

Teacher: _______ *is spelt* _______. (Teacher spells out the word, and pupils write the word on an index card.) *The word _____ can be broken up into ______ sounds. For example, "said" can be broken up into three sounds: /s/ /e/ /d/.*

Teacher raises one finger for each sound. Pupils are taught to repeat the teacher, raising a finger up for each sound.

Teacher and Pupils: Draw one dash on the card for each sound in the word. Teacher coaches pupils to say the sounds as they draw each line.

Teacher: (Teacher points to first dash.) *Which letter is making the sound* _____ (first sound)? (Teacher and pupils write the letter on the first dash. Teacher continues until arriving at the irregular part of the word.)

Teacher: (Points to dash for the irregular portion of word.) *This sound is ___, but in this word,* _______ (repeat heart word), *we spell the sound _______ with the letter(s) _______. This is what makes the word tricky. We have to remember these letters by heart, so I am going to draw a heart underneath.* (Teacher and pupil draw a heart under the dash and write the letter(s). Continue with the rest of the heart words.) *Let's read the heart word one more time.* (Pupils run their fingers under the word as they read it.) *What was the tricky part in _______?*

Pupils respond. Pupils add the index card to a card ring for later practice.

Additional Practice

Repeat procedure for additional words using the same prompts. The part of the word that is underlined is "irregular" and has to be memorised by heart.

Sound 1	Sound 2	Sound 3
/h/	/a/	/z/
h	a	**s**

Sound 1	Sound 2
/th/	/u/
th	**e**

Step 6: Practise Reading Sentences from the Text

The sentence reading portion of the lesson offers pupils an opportunity to practise integrating decoding, heart word and sight word skills. By selecting sentences from the text as a platform for practice, pupils can preview elements of the text before attempting to read the whole book.

Sentences for Game Plan

Sam sat on the mat.
"Sam, sit on it."
Tam sat on the mat.

Step 7: Expand Text-Related Vocabulary Knowledge

One key element of Structured Literacy routines is the integration of multiple aspects of word knowledge. This includes connecting knowledge about phonics with knowledge about word meaning. Several prominent theories of reading comprehension, including the Simple View of Reading (Gough & Tunmer, 1986) and the Reading Rope (Scarborough, 2001), highlight the fundamental role of vocabulary knowledge in reading achievement. By integrating a dedicated section for vocabulary instruction into each Game Plan, lessons support integrating a dedicated section for the development of sight word recognition, fluency and comprehension. Instruction that enhances both pupils' breadth of vocabulary knowledge and the number of associations they have for individual words strengthens word retrieval and supports text comprehension.

The vocabulary activity utilised in the current chapter's Game Plan is the same as the activity utilised in Chapter 1 (page 31). In order to enhance pupils' knowledge of word meanings, teachers can review previously taught words and incorporate a variety of questions that prompt pupils to think about word meanings. Questions may include references to synonyms, antonyms and characters in the story, or they may offer pupils opportunities to complete a sentence. Before the activity, display the words from the Single Word Reading portion of the Game Plan and lead pupils through a choral reading of the word list. See the table **Words and Questions for Vocabulary Activity** on page 55 for a demonstration of this activity in practice.

Words and Questions for Vocabulary Activity

Game Plan: *Sit, Sam*	**Questions**
Sam/Tam	Which words are names?
sit	Which word completes the blank in this sentence? I am tired and need to find a chair to ___ in.
sit	Which word is the opposite of stand? (sit)
sat	Which word completes the blank in this sentence? Yesterday, at the football game, we ___ in the stands.

Game Plan: *Pip, Sam and Tam*	**Questions**
Pip	Which word is a name?
tip	Which word means to fall over?
not	Which word has a negative meaning?
top	Which word means the peak, or highest level?

Maximise the Participation of All Pupils

In order to maximise the engagement of all pupils during vocabulary instruction, teachers can pair pupils together and instruct them in a "turn-and-talk" protocol. Turn-and-talk protocols teach pupils to take it in turns to share their ideas with each other.

Turn-and-talk is an efficient and effective engagement strategy as it means that 50 per cent of pupils are simultaneously answering each question. Compared with hand-raising, in which one pupil answers each question, turn-and-talk maximises opportunities for pupils to practise and learn with their peers.

How to Teach Kids to Turn-and-Talk

Early in primary school, many pupils struggle with impulse control and have difficulty waiting their turn to share their thinking. One reason hand-raising has become a universal tool for pupil engagement is because it gives pupils something to do as they signal to the teacher that they have a thought to share. However, as effective as hand-raising is at supporting impulse control, it is limited as a strategy for engagement. Only a portion of each class engages in regular hand-raising, and often the pupils who need the most support are the least likely to voluntarily participate in individual practice in front of their peers.

In order to support turn-and-talk as an effective alternative to hand-raising, teachers may need to explicitly teach pupils partner routines. The following ideas can support initial partner routines:

1. Assign consistent partners for different types of instruction. For example, during ELA instruction, pupils are paired with one talk partner, but during maths instruction, they might be paired with someone else. Pre-assigning partners can eliminate pupils' potential anxiety for needing to find their own partner and can lead to richer discussions among partnerships.

2. Model partner routines in front of the whole group with a low-risk conversation starter (e.g. one talk partner tells the other their favourite colour, etc.).

3. After practice, discuss what went well about the routine (e.g. turn-taking, quiet listening while partner speaks, keeping body quiet while partner speaks, facing partner and making eye contact as appropriate).

4. Continue to model, review and adjust turn-and-talk routines as necessary.

Step 8: Putting It All Together for Text Reading and Comprehension

In the final activities of the Game Plan, pupils must consolidate phonics skills and strategies, taught in isolation, to connected text. Before, during and after reading, pupils' comprehension is supported through a series of questions that support the connection between word reading and meaning-making. Prior to beginning reading, activate pupils' background knowledge about the text by reading the title, discussing the cover and previewing the content. In order to support comprehension monitoring, set a purpose for reading by posing one of the comprehension questions (e.g. "As we read, I want you to figure out the problem that our main character, _____, encounters in the book", or "Let's read to find out what happens to ____".).

Comprehension Questions for Game Plan

Factual
Who sat on the mat first?

Factual
Who sat on the mat last?

Inferential
Why did Tam ask Sam to sit on the mat?

Text from the Book *Sit, Sam*

Tam sat on the mat.

"Sam, sit on it."

"Sit, Sam, sit."

"Sit on it, Sam."

"Tam! Tam!"

Sam sat on the mat.

Use Choral or Partner Reading Instead of Round Robin

Maximising pupil engagement and participation ensures all pupils have adequate opportunities to build their reading skills. See Chapter 1 (page 32) to learn more about the three primary engagement techniques for book reading: choral reading, partner reading and reading to oneself.

Comprehension Questions

The comprehension questions developed for the Game Plans in this chapter focus on two aspects of text knowledge: factual knowledge and inferential knowledge. Factual questions are designed to support the recall and organisation of specific information from the text. Inferential questions are designed to support pupils' analysis of text, integrating facts from the story and background knowledge to provide rationale or explanations for behaviour.

Step 9: Applying Phonics Knowledge to Dictation

Although spelling patterns in English often feel nonsystematic and rife with irregularities, approximately 50 per cent of words in English can be spelt using common phonics rules, and an additional 30 per cent have only one sound with an irregular spelling (Moats & Tolman, 2009). Therefore, reinforcing common phonics rules through instructional routines that simultaneously practise key patterns in reading and spelling will increase the likelihood of consolidation and application among pupils. For example, learning to spell words enhances pupils' knowledge of the sound-symbol relationships that build sight word recognition, and when pupils spell words with phonics patterns targeted in their Structured Literacy routines, it enhances their decoding abilities (Graham et al, 2002; Moats, 2020).

Dictation Routine for Game Plan

Dictation	Selected Elements
Heart Word	the
Letters/Sounds/ Rime Patterns	-at, -it, -am
Words	sat, sit, Sam
Sentence	Sam sat on the mat.

WINNING STRATEGY: Reinforcing Word Recognition Through Spelling

Guided dictation is a Winning Strategy that supports both pupils' encoding and decoding skills. When it comes to planning the dictation portion, select an array of the sounds, words, heart words and sentences included in the Game Plan's reading activities. For the current Game Plan, the dictation activity includes one heart word, three individual sounds or rime patterns to spell, three words that feature the target phonics skills and one sentence. At times, it is necessary to simplify the sentence for dictation. In the current lesson, the sentence "Tam, Tim and Sam sat on it", can be changed from the original text to the dictation version, "Tim sat." Sentence adjustments will vary depending on the pupils' needs and the options from the text. Another common modification for dictation sentences is replacing pronouns with character names (e.g. "He sat"/"Tim sat"). Practising spelling characters' names helps reinforce the target phonics concept.

The dictation portion of the Game Plan is a wonderful opportunity to systematically teach the building blocks of spelling procedures in manageable increments. The sequence of activities moves from smaller to larger units of language, starting with sounds and words, then building to sentences. Furthermore, pupils are asked to spell sounds, words and sentences on the final day of the lesson sequence. By this time, they have already completed half a dozen reading activities with the same sounds, words and sentences. (See **Dictation Routine for Game Plan** on page 58.)

The dictation routine also offers an opportunity to provide explicit instruction in effective spelling strategies. Strategic spelling initially segments words into their smallest sound components. For example, breaking up a base word and its suffix, dividing syllables, or segmenting sounds. The letter(s) to spell each sound are then retrieved, and spelling rules are considered. The dictation approach is a modified version of Simultaneous Oral Spelling (SOS), a multisensory teaching procedure used to help pupils improve their spelling. By pronouncing each sound and corresponding letter before writing them down, pupils connect the phonological, visual and auditory processes needed for accurate spelling. The following **Teacher Script for Dictation with Corrective Feedback** on page 60 includes suggested teacher language for the routine. If your phonics curriculum has a dictation routine, feel free to utilise those resources in that portion of the routine.

Teacher Script for Dictation with Corrective Feedback

Introduction to Strategy

Teacher: *Now we are going to spell some sounds, rime patterns, words and write a sentence.*

Dictation of Heart Words

Teacher: *Your heart word to spell is _______.*

Pupils repeat the word.

The teacher can reinforce the Heart Word Magic strategy by identifying the number of sounds in the word and matching up the letters.

Prompt pupils as necessary.

Teacher: *How many sounds do you hear? What letter or letters represent that sound? Which letter or letters do we need to remember by heart?*

Corrective Feedback

If pupils incorrectly write the spelling for a sound or miss a letter (for example, if for the word "the" they write "tha"), use this script:

Teacher: *What's the word you are spelling?*

Pupil says word.

Have the pupil say the sounds and point to the letters that spell each sound.

When the pupil points to the incorrect letter(s), use this script:

Teacher: *You said _________. _________ is spelt ______ in the word _______.*

Pupil corrects misspelling.

Have the pupil say the sounds and point to the letters again to reinforce the correct spelling.

Pupils respond.

Dictation of Letters/Rime Patterns

For vowels and consonants:

Teacher: *The sound is _____.* (Pupils repeat the sound.)

Teacher: *What letter or letters make that sound?*

Pupils say and write the letter or letters.

For rime patterns:

Teacher: *The rime pattern is _____.*

Pupils repeat rime pattern.

Teacher: *What letters make the rime pattern?*

Pupils say and write the letters.

Corrective Feedback

If pupils respond incorrectly, use this script:

Teacher: *The sound (or rime pattern) is ____, and the letters that make that sound are _____.*

Pupils repeat.

Dictation of Single Words

Teacher: *The word is _____.* (Use the word in a sentence.)

Pupils repeat the word.

Teacher: *Tell me the starter sound in _____.*

Pupils provide.

Teacher: *What letter or letters make the starter sound?*

Pupils say and write the letter or letters.

Teacher: *Tell me the rime pattern in _____.*

Pupils provide.

Teacher: *What letters make the rime pattern?*

Pupils say and write the letters.

Teacher: *Read the word back to yourself and check that your letters match your sounds.*

This is a scaffolded approach. You can provide more or less support, depending on your pupils.

Corrective Feedback

If pupils respond incorrectly, use this script:

Teacher: *The sound (or rime pattern) is ____, and the letters that make that sound are ____.*

Pupils repeat.

Dictation of Sentences

Teacher: *The sentence is __________. Now, I am going to throw you the sentence. Hold your pencil in your writing hand and catch the sentence in your other hand.*

Mimic throwing the sentence, saying it again as you "throw" the words to the pupils.

Teacher: *Let the sentence out of your hand, putting up one finger for each word.*

Pupils follow the procedure, and the teacher ensures they have all of the words in the sentence.

After pupils have written the whole sentence, have them touch each word and read the sentence as they check for punctuation, missing words or spelling errors.

Corrective Feedback

For sentences longer than five words, consider breaking them into phrases and dictating each phrase separately. If pupils have difficulty remembering the sentence, remind/show them how to use their fingers to say the words.

Some pupils benefit from an additional scaffold of drawing a line for each word.

If pupils do not notice an error, have them point and read the sentence again. Show them the word with the error. If necessary, have them say the word, the sounds in the word and the letters that spell the sounds.

Proposed Practice Schedule

The nine-step routine outlined in this Game Plan is designed to be delivered over the course of several days. Delivering instruction in this manner not only creates a feasible schedule for teachers but also provides the opportunity for deliberate and spaced practice to support pupils in consolidating skills (Archer & Hughes, 2011). The practice schedule below provides suggestions for utilising the Game Plan in sessions ranging from 15–20 minutes. It should be noted that Day 1 does not include connected text practice. Providing daily opportunities to practise connected text is always preferable, so, if time permits, consider having pupils reread a familiar text from a previous lesson.

Day 1 (15 mins)	**Day 2 (18 mins)**	**Day 3 (17 mins)**
Phonemic Awareness (2 mins)	Building Knowledge of Heart Words (5 mins)	Book Reading and Comprehension Questions (7 mins)
Phonics Concept (5 mins)	Sentences (7 mins)	Dictation (10 mins)
Letter/Sound/Rime Review (3 mins)	Vocabulary (6 mins)	
Single Words (5 mins)		

Game Plan

Decodable Text: ***Pip, Sam and Tam*, Dandelion Readers Set 3 Units 1-10, Book 2**
Phonics Concept: **Rime pattern recognition of two- and three-letter short vowel words (VC and CVC)**

Phonemic Awareness			**Phonics Concept**
not	top	tip	Provide direct instruction in the phonics concept, utilising words pulled from the Reader and/or that fit the patterns you are teaching.
pit	Pip	Tam	

Letter/Sound/Rime Review

t	-an	-op	-ot	-ip	-am

Single Word Reading

not	top	tip	Pip

Heart Words

of	is

Sentence Reading

Tam is on top of Sam.

Pip, Tam and Sam tip.

Pip is not on top.

Vocabulary

Which word is a name? (Pip)	Which word means to fall over? (tip)	Which word has a negative meaning? (not)	Which word means the peak, or highest level? (top)

Story and Comprehension Questions

Who sat on top of Sam?	What happens when Pip gets on top?	Where did Pip, Sam and Tam land?

Dictation

Heart Word	of
Letters/Sounds/Rime Patterns	-op, -ot, -ip
Words	not, top, tip
Sentence	Pip is not on top.

Chapter 3

Early Sight Word Development

- Backwards decoding with complex rime patterns
- Utilising RAN charts to build automaticity with single words and phrases
- Developing word associations through vocabulary instruction

Game Plan

Decodable Text: ***Junk*, Dandelion Launchers Units 8-10, Book 8c**
Phonics Concept: **Rime pattern recognition of short vowel words with final adjacent consonants (CVCC)**

Phonemic Awareness			Phonics Concept
must	tent	went	Provide direct instruction in the phonics concept, utilising words pulled from the Reader and/or that fit the patterns you are teaching.
dump	camp	junk	

Letter/Sound/Rime Review

-amp	-ank	-ump	-ent	-ust	-unk

Single Word Reading

must	went	dump	camp

Heart Words

said	the	to	of

RAN Charts (Single Words & Phrases)

must	went	camp	dump	at the dump	off to camp	this old tent	I must
went	camp	dump	must	off to camp	this old tent	I must	at the dump
camp	must	went	dump	this old tent	off to camp	at the dump	I must
dump	went	camp	must	I must	at the dump	off to camp	this old tent

Sentence Reading

"I must get rid of this old tent," said Alf.

Alf met Hank at the dump.

Hank and Alf went off to camp.

Vocabulary: mend

Definition	Sentence	Questions
(v) To repair something.	My sister used her sewing kit to mend the hole in my shirt.	Why would you need to mend something? What tools can you use to mend? What is another word for mend?

Story & Comprehension Questions

What does Alf bring to the dump?	Why did Alf bring the tent to the dump?	In the story, Hank offers to mend a tent. What skills does Hank need to mend the tent? What other word means the same as "mend"?

Dictation

Heart Word	said
Letters/Sounds/Rime Patterns	-ust, -ent, -amp
Words	must, went, camp
Sentence	Alf met Hank at the dump.

Target Skills for Game Plan

In the Partial Mapping Phase of word recognition, pupils continue to build skills in order to become automatic in their ability to recognise larger units of language. When pupils are able to attend to larger word parts, such as adjacent consonants and rime patterns, they are more efficient in mapping and have greater automaticity in reading. Some pupils require additional instruction and practice opportunities in order to move to the final word recognition phase of reading, Consolidated Alphabetic/ Orthographic Mapping. The activities and instruction in the Game Plan aid in developing the following skill:

- Automatic recognition of four-letter short vowel words with final adjacent consonants (CVCC)

Your Team

Pupils who are able to accurately blend sounds together to read three-letter short vowel words are ready for this lesson. Pupils may even be able to read some CVC words automatically or by rime pattern or be accurately blending the sounds for four-letter short vowel words. Typically, pupils achieve this skill at the Reception level. However, pupils in any phase or year group can benefit from these strategies if they still rely on sound-by-sound reading and have yet to build their "sight word vocabulary" to instantly recognise words as a whole unit.

Case Study

Sienna is in Reception and knows the letters and corresponding sounds of the alphabet. She can read and spell many CVC words and heart words with automaticity, but at times she resorts back to reading words sound by sound. Sienna's teacher has been meeting with her in a small group for several weeks. The instruction has focused on introducing backwards decoding, or reading by rime pattern. Sienna's teacher reports she is utilising this strategy in the small group but might benefit from additional practice in order to apply it independently to longer words. What strategies/activities can the teacher use to move Sienna towards more independence?

Resources for Skill Identification

Many pupils acquire the skills needed to read and spell VC and CVC words with strong whole class Structured Literacy, but they struggle when words become more complex (for example, when adding adjacent consonants at the beginning and end of short vowel words). As instruction increases in complexity, pupils' skills may begin to diverge, and some may require robust small group instruction. In order to plan and deliver instruction that meets pupils' needs, utilise materials to identify appropriate instructional focus areas. There are several resources available to educators; these include the phonics progression of your core classroom instruction and/or diagnostic assessment tools.

Phonics Progression from Classroom Curriculum

The phonics progression from your classroom curriculum can be an effective tool for identifying a target skill when your pupils are only slightly below the expected level and demonstrate similar learning needs/profiles. For example, after completing a unit on digraphs such as 'ch', 'th' and 'sh', a small group of pupils continue to mispronounce the sound of short vowel /i/. This is a skill that was introduced and practised in the previous unit. As you plan your small group intervention, focus on passages or books with plentiful opportunities to read short vowel /i/ words, rather than moving ahead in the phonics progression to focus on digraphs.

Phonics Assessment

Diagnostic tools such as phonics assessments are particularly helpful when there is a group of pupils with varying levels of ability. They are also useful in situations where an established phonics progression is unavailable. Diagnostic tools function as inventories in identifying skills that are "in stock" versus those that need to be taught or mastered. Most assessments present a collection of individual letter sounds, sight words and sentences for pupils to read. Examiners tally the raw scores and analyse error patterns to determine target skills for instruction. Commonly used phonics assessments include the EYFS profile (Department for Education, 2024) and the Year 1 Phonics Screening Check (Standards and Testing Agency, 2012).

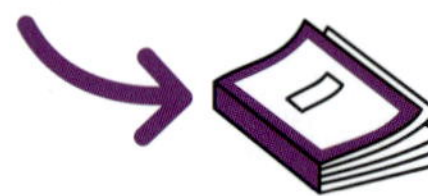

Your Equipment

Series: Dandelion Launchers Units 8-10 (ISBN 9781907170348)

Reader: *Junk* (Book 8c)

Phonics Concept: Rime pattern recognition of short vowel words with final adjacent consonants (CVCC).

Book Overview: Two strangers share common interests in upcycling and outdoor activities.

Text from the Book *Junk*

"I must get rid of this old tent," said Alf.

Alf went to the dump.

Alf met Hank at the dump.

"I can mend that old tent," said Hank.

"I can mend that old lamp," said Alf.

Hank and Alf went off to camp.

Additional Texts

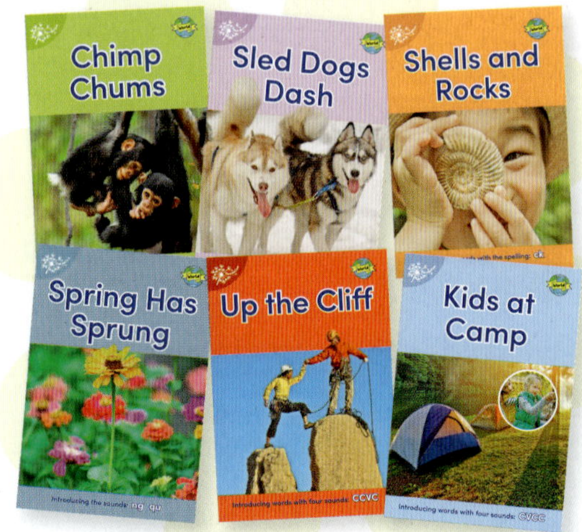

Dandelion World Stages 8-15 (9780241666708) follows the same phonics progression as **Dandelion Launchers Units 8-10**, thereby providing the opportunity for instruction in additional texts.

An additional Game Plan that targets similar skills and utilises another book from the **Dandelion Launchers Units 8-10** series is available at the end of the chapter.

Planning for Game Day

The Game Plan for Chapter 3 was designed using a backwards planning approach. Planning lessons with the end in mind – application of skills to connected text – ensures that skill-building activities in the Structured Literacy routines prioritise patterns, vocabulary and text pupils will encounter in the accompanying book. The sequence for backwards planning is shared in the following breakout box on page 69.

Backwards Planning Using a Decodable Text

Planning Reading Activities (Sentences, Single Words, RAN Charts and Letter Sounds)

Step 1: Choose three sentences from the text. Select sentences that offer practice for target phonics skills.

Step 2: Select four individual words that appear in the sentences for single word reading practice.

Step 3: To build RAN charts, use the four individual words and appropriate short phrases from the sentences.

Step 4: Choose letters and rime patterns from the single word practice to teach sound-symbol correspondence.

Planning Phonemic Awareness Activity

Use the words from the Single Word Reading activity for phonemic awareness (blending).

Planning Heart Word and Dictation Activity

Step 1: Choose up to four heart words from the text.

Step 2: Select rime patterns, one heart word, three single words and at least one sentence from the reading activities for dictation tasks.

Planning Vocabulary and Comprehension Activities

Step 1: Select a high-utility word from the book and develop 'w' questions to elicit pupils' connections or associations.

Step 2: Read the text and craft questions that require pupils to find the information in the text (factual questions), analyse word meaning (semantic questions) or "read between the lines" to understand the deeper purpose of the text (inference questions). Set a purpose for reading by providing a question for pupils to keep in mind as they read the book.

Winning Strategies

The instructional routines in the Game Plan for this chapter support the ongoing development of pupils' word recognition skills. This is achieved through the utilisation of the following three Winning Strategies:

- Backwards decoding with complex rime patterns
- Utilising RAN charts to build automaticity with single words and phrases
- Developing word associations through vocabulary instruction

Backwards Decoding

One of the Winning Strategies covered in Chapter 2 (page 47) introduced pupils to the concept of reading by rime pattern, otherwise referred to as backwards decoding. A rime pattern consists of the vowel and any subsequent consonants within that word, or in multisyllabic words, that syllable. For example, in the word "junk", the rime pattern is "-unk" and the starter, or onset, is 'j'.

Backwards decoding is particularly effective as pupils move from reading three- to four-sound words. The new sound places additional cognitive demands on pupils' auditory memory. As a result, many children struggle to accurately sequence and pronounce four- and five-letter words. Common errors include omitting a sound (e.g. "but" for "bunt"), switching the position of sounds (e.g. "felt" for "left") or mispronouncing sounds (e.g. "punt" for "pant"). Backwards decoding reduces the frequency with which these errors occur by utilising phonological, or auditory, memory. Phonological memory is part of the phonological processor, one of the four interconnected systems (e.g. phonological, orthographic, semantic and contextual processors) that make meaning out of written language (Seidenberg & McClelland, 1989). Backwards decoding with single-syllable words can provide the foundation necessary for pupils when they encounter words with more complex rime patterns, as well as words with two or more syllables.

Utilising RAN Charts to Build Automaticity with Single Words and Phrases

As noted in Chapter 2, the use of rime pattern instruction supports pupils' ability to move away from decoding words one sound at a time and towards recognising them as a whole unit. Rapid Automatic Naming (RAN) charts provide a repeated presentation of single words or phrases from the text. The use of a RAN chart offers several benefits. First, it provides an opportunity to practise the automatic retrieval of common single words and phrases. Second, it supports tracking across the page and the "return sweep" to the next line (Wolf & Katzir-Cohen, 2001). By incorporating backwards decoding and the use of RAN charts, educators provide the scaffolds sometimes necessary to move pupils away from reading sound by sound and towards automatic recognition of words as a whole unit. Automatic word recognition, or "sight word recognition", indicates the word has been processed so efficiently by the pupil's reading circuit that it is now instantly recognisable, or orthographically mapped. The instant recognition of orthographically mapped words is essential for overall reading achievement. Decoding every word diminishes reading fluency and comprehension of text.

Developing Word Associations Through Vocabulary Instruction

Vocabulary instruction is an important element in building word recognition and fluency skills, as words with a greater number of associations are recognised more quickly in printed text (Pexman et al, 2008). There are several different features of word meaning that enhance associations and subsequent retrieval. Notably, vocabulary words that have more "semantic neighbours", or associations, that frequently co-occur in the same content are retrieved more quickly than words with fewer neighbours. For example, the word "pitch" co-occurs with words such as football, sports, player, sales and cricket. By contrast, the word "mulch" tends to co-occur with fewer words, such as garden, dirt and leaves. Building the density of pupils' semantic neighbourhoods is an important part of vocabulary instruction. In the Game Plan, vocabulary instruction combines explicit instruction and guided questioning designed to elicit experiences about the features of key vocabulary terms.

Executing Your Game Plan

Step 1: Maximise Phonemic Awareness Instruction

Our ability to recognise, identify and manipulate individual sounds in spoken words is called phonemic awareness. Phonemic awareness activities that have high utility include blending and segmenting. These skills are the most closely related to our ability to decode and encode. In the Game Plan, the words used in the phonemic awareness activities are pulled directly from the text and address the lesson's target phonics skills. If the text offers a limited selection of practice words, bolster your activity with additional words that follow your target pattern. See Chapter 1 (pages 24–25) for the **Teacher Script for Introducing, Modelling and Practising Phonemic Awareness**.

Words for Phonemic Awareness Blending Activity in Game Plan

Sounds to Blend	Whole Word
/m/ /u/ /s/ /t/	must
/t/ /e/ /n/ /t/	tent
/w/ /e/ /n/ /t/	went
/d/ /u/ /m/ /p/	dump
/k/ /a/ /m/ /p/	camp
/j/ /u/ /n/ /k/	junk

Step 2: Teach Phonics Concepts Using Winning Strategies

The target phonics skill for the Game Plan is the automatic recognition of four-letter short vowel words with final adjacent consonants. Select several CVCC words from the decodable text to use for instruction in the Winning Strategies.

WINNING STRATEGY: Backwards Decoding with Complex Rime Patterns

In order to achieve the Game Plan's phonics goal, the lesson incorporates the Winning Strategy of backwards decoding. Backwards decoding moves pupils towards greater automaticity in recognising letter pattern chunks. During backwards decoding, pupils are prompted to read words in the following sequence:

1. Pronounce the rime pattern
2. Pronounce the starter sound
3. Blend the starter and the rime pattern
4. Re-pronounce the whole word

As noted earlier, this technique may be useful for pupils who continue to read most words sound by sound and may be helpful to move pupils to partially mapping words.

Differentiating Instruction to Offer Increased Support

Some pupils may struggle to accurately read rime patterns that include two final consonant sounds. In these cases, teachers can break down the task in order to offer more incremental support. This process involves breaking up the final adjacent consonants and modelling reading the rime pattern with the first consonant, pronouncing the second consonant in isolation, then blending the entire rime pattern before adding the starter sound.

1. hunt:	/un/	- /t/	- /unt/	- /h/	- hunt
2. tent:	/en/	- /t/	- /ent/	- /t/	- tent
3. left:	/ef/	- /t/	- /eft/	- /l/	- left

Rebellious Rime Patterns

There are some English rime patterns in short vowel words that do not follow the rules. We call them rebellious rime patterns. The letter sounds rebel against short vowel conventions by making a long vowel sound or a distorted nasal vowel sound.

Step-by-Step Instruction for Teaching Rebellious Rime Patterns

Rebellious rime patterns should always be taught as a unit, as dividing them will elicit a mispronunciation of the vowel sound. Pupils benefit from explicit instruction with the pronunciation of rebellious rime patterns as they are unexpected and require additional explanation, modelling and practice.

Teacher Script for Modelling and Practising Backwards Decoding with Complex Rime Patterns

Introduction to Strategy

Teacher: *Let's continue using our backwards decoding strategy and reading words by rime pattern first. You might notice the rime patterns in these words are a little longer than we are used to. We have to teach our brains to read across longer words.*

Type of Words

Single-Syllable Short Vowel Words with Final Adjacent Consonants (CVCC Words)

Teacher Language and Prompt for Modelling

Write "such" and underline the rime pattern.

Teacher: *Watch me read the rime pattern: "-uch". Now I pronounce the starter sound: "s-". Finally, I blend them together: "such". I repeat the whole word: "such".*

Repeat the procedure with pupils, simplifying language.

Teacher: *Rime pattern.* (Elicit "-uch".)
Starter sound. (Elicit "s-".)
Blend. (Elicit /s/ /u/ /ch/.)
Whole word. (Elicit "such".)

Additional Practice

Repeat the procedure for additional words using the same prompts. As a teacher, be sure to write the words without reading them aloud.

1. pick: /ick/ - /p/ - pick
2. sock: /ock/ - /s/ - sock
3. much: /uch/ - /m/ - much
4. gulp: /ulp/ - /g/ - gulp

Common Rebellious Rime Patterns

all - "fall"
am - "jam"
an - "can"
ang - "fang"
ank - "tank"

ild - "child"
ind - "mind"

old - "cold"
oll - "roll"
ost - "most"

Teacher Script for Modelling and Practising Backwards Decoding with Rebellious Rime Patterns

Introduction to Strategy

Teacher: *Let's continue with reading words using backwards decoding. Today, we are going to start learning about some patterns that "rebel", or break phonics rules we have been learning. We will call them rebellious rime patterns.*

Type of Words

Single-Syllable Short Vowel Words with Rebellious Rime Pattern (CVCC Words)

Teacher Language and Prompt for Modelling

Write the word "fall" on the board and underline the rime pattern "-all".

Teacher: *Our rebellious rime pattern today is A-L-L. The keyword to remember the pattern is "fall", and we pronounce the rime pattern as "-all". Now let's practise together.*

Teacher: *Letters.* (Elicit "A-L-L".)
Keyword. (Elicit "fall".)
Rime pattern. (Elicit "-all".)
Let's practise backwards decoding words that contain our new rebellious rime pattern.

Additional Practice

Repeat the procedure for additional rebellious rime patterns using the same prompts. Suggested keywords and additional pattern practice items are included:

Rebellious Rime	Keyword	Additional Items for Practice
-all	fall	tall, mall, ball
-am	jam	ram, ham, Sam
-ind	mind	find, kind, bind
-old	cold	told, fold, bold

Step 3: Reinforce Letters/Sounds in Isolation

The Game Plan includes activities for practising rime patterns. Teaching familiar letter patterns such as rime units enables greater automaticity in word recognition and spelling. The Game Plan features six rime patterns featured in decodable words in the story *Junk*. See Chapter 1 (page 28) for **Teacher Script for Introducing, Modelling and Practising Letter/ Sound Review** as necessary.

Rime Patterns for Game Plan

-amp	-ank	-ump
-ent	-ust	-unk

Step 4: Apply Phonics Concept to Single Words from the Text

The Game Plan features four words from the story *Junk* and the sentences from which they have been taken. The rime patterns that comprise the selected words offer practice with the lesson's target phonics skill (i.e. reading short vowel words with final adjacent consonants). Apply the instructional language from the **Teacher Script for Modelling and Practising Backwards Decoding with Complex Rime Patterns** (page 73) to practise the single words from *Junk*.

Once your pupils have been introduced to the concept of backwards decoding complex rime patterns (see page 72), you will want to provide ample opportunities for direct and explicit practice.

Individual Words for Game Plan

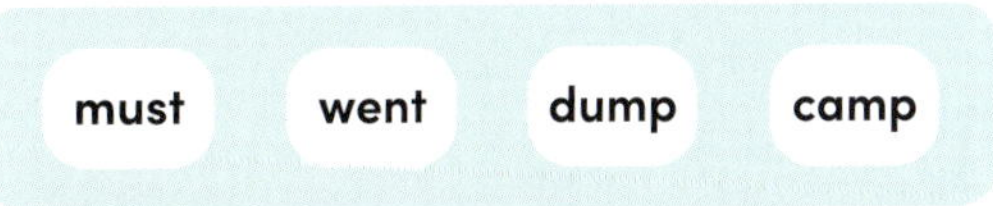

must | went | dump | camp

Step 5: Build Knowledge of Heart Words

The Game Plan for this chapter features four heart words from the decodable story *Junk*. See Chapter 2 (pages 52–53) for the **Teacher Script for Modelling and Practising Reading and Writing Heart Words** if needed.

The format that teachers can use to demonstrate dividing the heart words by sound and the irregular aspect of the words is outlined below.

Heart Words for Game Plan

As a teacher, be sure to model breaking the words into sounds and matching letters for each sound. The part of the word indicated by the heart is "irregular" and therefore has to be memorised by heart.

Sound 1	Sound 2	Sound 3
/s/	/e/	/d/
s	**ai**	d

Sound 1	Sound 2
/th/	/u/
th	**e**

Sound 1	Sound 2
/t/	/oo/
t	**o**

Sound 1	Sound 2
/u/	/v/
o	**f**

Step 6: Enhance Sight Word Recognition with RAN Charts

The Game Plan features one RAN chart of single words and one chart of phrases. Both the single words and phrases have been practised in earlier Game Plan activities. By providing a repeated presentation of these elements, the RAN charts offer a platform for enhancing sight word vocabulary through rapid recognition.

Maximising Pupil Engagement with RAN Charts

The RAN charts in the Game Plan consist of both the individual words in isolation and short phrases from the sentences and text. RAN charts are intended to be read chorally to maximise the participation of all members of the group. Choral reading of RAN charts is achieved by displaying one copy of the chart, digitally or in print, and controlling the pacing of reading with nonverbal cues, or "sweeps", under the word or phrase. It may be helpful for teachers to use the scripts for RAN chart instruction and error correction on pages 78–79.

RAN Charts for Game Plan

at the dump	off to camp	this old tent	I must
off to camp	this old tent	I must	at the dump
this old tent	off to camp	at the dump	I must
I must	at the dump	off to camp	this old tent

must	went	camp	dump
went	camp	dump	must
camp	must	went	dump
dump	went	camp	must

WINNING STRATEGY: Utilising RAN Charts to Build Automaticity with Single Words and Phrases

The RAN charts are used to reinforce automatic word recognition, and if pupils continue to decode words sound by sound when reading the RAN chart, educators may want to revisit individual word reading and backwards decoding activities. RAN charts are common tools used in cognitive neuroscience to ascertain the rate at which individuals can pair symbols with their verbal language (Wolf & Denckla, 2005). A traditional RAN chart randomly presents an array of five different objects, letters or numbers across a page in four or five consecutive rows. The time it takes an individual to name all the symbols is highly correlated with their overall reading rate, or fluency. When used with younger children, it is a helpful predictive measure and indicates risk of later challenges with reading fluency. Practising traditional object, letter or number RAN charts has no academic value. Yet, RAN charts populated with frequently occurring words, letter patterns or common phrases provide the repetition and practice necessary for some pupils to develop automatic word retrieval skills as they read across a line of text (Wolf et al, 2009).

Teacher Script for Modelling and Practising RAN Chart Reading with Corrective Feedback

Introduction to Strategy

Teacher: *Now we are going to see the words we have been reading individually repeated in the rows of this chart. We are going to read the chart together, and all our voices will blend like a chorus.*

RAN Chart Examples

must	went	camp	dump
went	camp	dump	must
camp	must	went	dump
dump	went	camp	must

at the dump	off to camp	this old tent	I must
off to camp	this old tent	I must	at the dump
this old tent	off to camp	at the dump	I must
I must	at the dump	off to camp	this old tent

Teacher Feedback

Teacher: *When I put my pointer to the left of the word/phrase, think of it in your head. When I scoop underneath, say it aloud. Watch me.* (Demonstrate reading words/phrases in first three boxes.)

Corrective Feedback

When pupils pronounce a word or phrase inaccurately on the RAN chart, provide immediate corrective feedback using the following sequence:

Teacher: *My turn. That word is* ______.
Your turn. (Elicit choral response from pupils accurately pronouncing the word.)

Then, move the pointer back two squares to provide another opportunity for correct pronunciation.

For persistent errors, teachers can reteach target phonics skills by modelling the strategy and offering plentiful opportunities for practice.

Tips for Differentiating RAN Chart Instruction

If the skills of your pupils vary significantly, then you may want to use some of the differentiation strategies listed below.

Colour-Code a RAN Chart

One way to differentiate the RAN chart is by colour-coding rows to align with pupils' needs. For example, pupils reading rows shaded red may benefit from complete word practice, while pupils reading from rows shaded yellow may be practising individual letter sounds or rime patterns in isolation. It is most beneficial for each pupil to read at least two rows to practise the "return sweep", the eye movement that allows the reader to fixate on the next line of text.

It may be helpful to provide each pupil with their own copy of the RAN chart.

Customise a RAN Chart

Readers who are slowly building foundational skills may benefit from a simple RAN chart that includes one or two words and common letter patterns (for example, a common rime pattern) from those words.

must	went	camp	dump
went	camp	dump	must

Supporting Multilingual Pupils

After reading the first line of a RAN chart, it may be beneficial to review the meaning of each word by using them in sentences, displaying a related image or illustration or asking pupils to pantomime their connection to the word.

Step 7: Practise Reading Sentences from the Text

The sentence reading portion of the lesson offers pupils an opportunity to practise integrating decoding, heart word and sight word skills. By selecting sentences from the text as a platform for practice, pupils can preview elements of the story. Additionally, supported repeated reading of connected text aids with the development of fluency and prosody skills. The current Game Plan has selected the following sentences from the text *Junk* because they include words that have final adjacent consonants in the rime pattern (e.g. tent, must, dump, camp, Hank).

Sentences for Game Plan

"I must get rid of this old tent," said Alf.

Alf met Hank at the dump.

Hank and Alf went off to camp.

Step 8: Expand Text-Related Vocabulary Knowledge

The vocabulary activities incorporated into Game Plans support the development of word recognition and are related to the text. As noted in the earlier chapters, vocabulary instruction is an important element in building pupils' word recognition. The vocabulary instruction in this chapter shifts away from defining multiple words to increasing pupils' depth of knowledge about a single word. The word "mend" is used for all vocabulary discussion and questions in the current Game Plan.

Vocabulary Word for Game Plan

Vocabulary Term
mend
Pupil-Friendly Definition
To repair something. (verb)
Using the Term in a Sentence
My sister used her sewing kit to mend the hole in my shirt.
Questions for Discussion:

- Why would you need to mend something?
- What tools can you use to mend?
- What is another word for mend?

WINNING STRATEGY: Developing Word Associations Through Vocabulary Instruction

The number of associations pupils have for a single vocabulary word is often referred to as their "semantic neighbourhood" (Buchanan et al, 1996). Uniformly dense neighbourhoods are common among pupils with strong background knowledge or literacy exposure. Pupils may also possess uneven neighbourhood density that is only clustered around certain topics or types of vocabulary. For example, some pupils know a great deal about football but have minimal knowledge about Africa. The density of a word's semantic neighbourhood can be developed through a combination of explicit instruction and guided questioning designed to elicit experiences about the features of key vocabulary terms. Guided questions utilise keywords such as *who, what, when, where* and *how* to elicit pupils' associations and support the visualisation of the vocabulary word in real life.

Step-by-Step Approach to Developing Word Associations Through Vocabulary Instruction

In order to develop a robust semantic neighbourhood for a word, follow a simple sequence. First, provide a child-friendly definition and illustration of the term. Then, present the word in context by featuring it in a sentence. Finally, engage pupils with questions that elicit and develop associations and enhance visualisation and imagery (see **Suggested Teacher Language for Building Word Associations** on page 82 for examples). When used in combination, visualisation and the development of rich semantic neighbourhoods have a positive impact on automatic word retrieval (Yap et al, 2012).

Suggested Teacher Language for Building Word Associations

Vocabulary Term

rid

Pupil-Friendly Definition

To remove someone or something completely. (verb)

Using the Term in a Sentence

Alf wants to get rid of his old tent.

Questions for Discussion

- Have you ever got rid of old items?
- Why did you need to get rid of them?
- Where did you put them?

Vocabulary Term

tent

Pupil-Friendly Definition

A shelter that can be used for sleeping. It is usually made of fabric and held up with poles or ropes. (noun)

Using the Term in a Sentence

The tent kept our family dry while camping in the rain.

Questions for Discussion

- When do you use a tent?
- How does it feel to sleep inside a tent?
- What supplies might you have in a tent?
- Who or what might you want to keep out of a tent?

Selecting Vocabulary Words

Vocabulary selection for your Game Plan is often subjective. In a Structured Literacy routine, the primary criterion is choosing a word that exemplifies the target phonics concept. However, several other vocabulary options likely exist in your text. Teachers might select a word because it is related to other academic topics and supports continuity of learning. Other vocabulary choices may connect to the knowledge and experiences of your pupils. For example, pupils who live in areas with waterways may be more familiar with the term "punting" and its associated boating activities than those who live in more mountainous or urban areas. One helpful rule of thumb is selecting words that are commonly occurring in text and used across disciplines but not often utilised in spoken language. Such vocabulary has been called "Tier 2" and is often unfamiliar to pupils but thought to be more utilitarian than content-specific vocabulary (Beck et al, 2013).

Step 9: Putting It All Together for Text Reading and Comprehension

Ultimately, building word recognition skills is a pathway to ensuring fluent reading and comprehension. Although decodable texts are short and often limited in content, the passages still present opportunities to practise multiple aspects of pupils' comprehension, including factual, inferential and vocabulary knowledge. The following questions have been generated for the Game Plan.

Comprehension Questions for Game Plan

Factual
What does Alf bring to the dump?

Inferential
Why did Alf bring the tent to the dump?

Vocabulary in Context
In the story, Hank offers to mend a tent.
What skills does Hank need to mend the tent?
What other word means the same as "mend"?

Text from the Book *Junk*
"I must get rid of this old tent," said Alf.
Alf went to the dump.
Alf met Hank at the dump.
"I can mend that old tent," said Hank.
"I can mend that old lamp," said Alf.
Hank and Alf went off to camp.

For the book reading portion, see Chapter 1 (pages 29 and 32) to learn more about maximising pupil engagement during this portion of the lesson.

Step 10: Applying Phonics Knowledge to Dictation

The development of spelling skills often lags behind the development of reading skills, and pupils benefit from the implementation of a comprehensive approach that simultaneously supports the development of phonics skills for both word reading and spelling (Graham, 2020).

In Chapter 2 (page 45), a modified Simultaneous Oral Spelling routine is introduced. This is a way for teachers to ensure that pupils are taught astrategic, incremental approach to spelling. The Teacher Scripts and recommendations for differentiated instruction from Chapter 2 can be referred to as needed. A selection of rime patterns, words and sentences used for reading have been featured in the dictation portion of the Game Plan.

Dictation Routine for Game Plan

Dictation	Selected Elements
Heart Word	said
Letters/Sounds/ Rime Patterns	-ust, -ent, -amp
Words	must, went, camp
Sentence	Alf met Hank at the dump.

Proposed Practice Schedule

An instructional lesson with 10+ steps is logistically impossible for most teachers to deliver in one sitting. The practice schedule below suggests one method of arranging the activities into approximately 20-minute lessons over the course of three days. As the first day of the lesson does not include connected text practice, rereading previously learnt sentences for a quick lesson warm-up is recommended.

Day 1 (20 mins)	Day 2 (22 mins)	Day 3 (20 mins)
Phonemic Awareness (2 mins)	Heart Words (5 mins)	RAN Chart – Phrases (5 mins)
Phonics Concept (5 mins)	Sentences (5 mins)	Dictation (10 mins)
Letter/Sound/Rime Review (3 mins)	Vocabulary (5 mins)	Finish Book/ Read Another Book (5 mins)
Single Words (5 mins)	Book Reading (read portion/entire book) (7 mins)	
RAN Chart – Single Words (5 mins)		

Game Plan

Decodable Text: ***The Gift*, Dandelion Launchers Stages Units 8-10, Book 8d**
Phonics Concept: **Rime pattern recognition of short vowel words with final adjacent consonants (CVCC)**

Phonemic Awareness			Phonics Concept
felt	gift	must	Provide direct instruction in the phonics concept, utilising words pulled from the Reader and/or that fit the patterns you are teaching.
damp	hand	tank	

Letter/Sound/Rime Review

-elt	-ift	-ust	-amp	-ank	-ad

Single Word Reading

felt	gift	damp	tank

RAN Charts (Single Words and Phrases)

felt	gift	damp	tank	the gift	with his hand	cold and damp	in a tank
gift	damp	tank	felt	with his hand	cold and damp	in a tank	the gift
damp	tank	felt	gift	cold and damp	in a tank	the gift	with his hand
tank	felt	gift	damp	in a tank	the gift	with his hand	cold and damp

Heart Words

you	cold	said	live

Sentence Reading

Alf felt the gift with his hand.

"It is cold and damp!" Alf said.

"It must live in a tank," said Dad.

Vocabulary: tank

Definition	Sentence	Questions
(n) A large receptacle for holding liquid (or gas), usually for animals to live in.	We need a tank for the three fish we just bought at the pet shop.	What different animals live in tanks? What are some important things to consider when buying a tank for an animal?

Story and Comprehension Questions

How did Alf describe the gift his dad gave him?	What hint did Alf's dad give him?	When Alf is trying to guess the gift, he says it is cold and damp. What does the word "damp" mean?

Dictation

Heart Word	you
Letters/Sounds/Rime Patterns	-elt, -ift, -amp
Words	felt, gift, damp
Sentence	It must live in a tank.

Chapter 4

Building Stamina with Longer Words

- Backwards decoding with initial adjacent consonants and digraphs
- Reading and spelling with suffix -s
- Expanding vocabulary knowledge with multiple-meaning words

Game Plan

Decodable Text: ***Chips for Lunch*, Dandelion Readers Set 2 Units 11-20, Book 11**
Phonics Concept: **Short vowel rime patterns with initial adjacent consonants or digraphs (CCVC); suffix -s**

Phonemic Awareness			**Phonics Concept**
grass	pinch	smelt	Provide direct instruction in the phonics concept, utilising words pulled from the Reader and/or that fit the patterns you are teaching.
bench	plank	chips	

Letter/Sound/Rime Review

gr-	sm-	pl-	-ank	ch-	-elt

Suffix Review

-s

Single Word Reading

grass	plank	smelt	chips

Heart Words

the	were	said	put

RAN Charts (Single Words and Phrases)

grass	plank	smelt	chips	on the grass	smelt the chips	on the plank	pinch the chips
plank	grass	chips	smelt	smelt the chips	on the grass	pinch the chips	on the plank
smelt	chips	grass	plank	on the plank	pinch the chips	on the grass	smelt the chips
chips	plank	smelt	grass	pinch the chips	smelt the chips	on the plank	on the grass

Sentence Reading

Chen put the chess set on the grass.

Pip and Tess smelt the chips.

Tess and Pip got up on to the plank to pinch the chips from the bag.

Multiple-Meaning Word: plank

Definition 1 (n) A long, thick board.	**Definition 2** (n) An exercise where you support your outstretched, face-down body with your arms and toes.	**Questions** What does planking look like? Why might this exercise move be called a plank? What are some things you need a plank of wood for?
Sentence 1 The carpenter grabbed the plank of wood from the back of his truck.	**Sentence 2** The instructor ended the exercise class with a series of planks.	

Story and Comprehension Questions

Why did Chen leave the chips on the bench?	How do Pip and Tess get to the chips?	How do you think Chen and Liz feel at the end of the story?

Dictation

Heart Word	put
Letters/Sounds/Rime Patterns	gr-, pl-, sm-
Words	grass, plank, chips
Sentence	Pip and Tess smelt the chips.

Target Skills for Game Plan

In Chapter 3, instruction focused on building pupils' reading skills as they move from the Full Alphabetic/Decoding Phase to automatically recognising larger chunks of four-letter short vowel words. The ability to read words by larger chunks is referred to as Partial Mapping and serves as a critical midpoint as pupils move away from sound-by-sound reading to recognising words instantaneously. In Chapter 4, this work continues with increasingly complex patterns and longer words. Increases in word length are due to several factors. These factors include the addition of adjacent consonants (e.g. bl, sp, st) or digraphs (e.g. ch, wh, sh) at the beginning of the word and the addition of suffixes at the end.

The activities and instruction in the Game Plan aid in developing the following skills:

- Automatic recognition of four- and five-letter short vowel words with initial adjacent consonants or digraphs
- Automatic recognition of all short vowel words with the addition of the suffix -s
- Spelling all short vowel words with the addition of the suffix -s

Your Team

Pupils are ready for this lesson structure when they are able to automatically recognise some short vowel rime patterns (-VC), including those that end with adjacent consonants (-VCC). Pupils should also be able to correctly pronounce consonant digraphs (e.g. ch, sh) in isolation. Typically, pupils achieve this skill at the end of Reception. However, pupils in any phase or year group will benefit from these strategies if they continue to rely on sound-by-sound reading and have yet to develop reading fluency with taught concepts.

Case Study

Jonah is a Reception pupil who is developing his word reading skills. When reading CVC words, he is largely accurate, but his teacher notices that when Jonah encounters longer short vowel words, his reading becomes inaccurate. When words contain adjacent consonants, he is able to segment the sounds correctly, but when he recodes (blends) individual sounds into a word, he is incorrect. Jonah also often leaves off the endings of words. When spelling, Jonah consistently omits consonant sounds that are part of a blend. What strategies/activities can help move Jonah towards more independence?

Your Equipment

Series: Dandelion Readers Set 2 Units 11-20 (ISBN 9781907170065)
Reader: *Chips for Lunch* (Book 11)
Phonics Concept: Recognition of short vowel words with initial adjacent consonants or digraphs (CCVC and CCVCC); suffix -s.
Book Overview: Two naughty ants wreak havoc on Chen and Liz's day of food and fun at the park.

Text from the Book *Chips for Lunch*

Chen and Liz went to get chips for lunch. The chips were hot. Chen left the chips on the bench.

"Let's get the chess set," said Liz. "I am a champ at chess." Chen put the chess set on the grass.

Pip and Tess smelt the chips. "Let's pinch the chips," said Pip. Pip got a plank and set it up.

Tess and Pip got up on to the plank to pinch the chips from the bag. Bad ants!

The bugs sat on the grass. "Let's chomp on the chips," said Pip. Yum! Yum!

Chen and Liz got up and sat on the bench. "Just six chips left! The ants got the chips!" yelled Chen.

Additional Texts

An additional Game Plan that targets similar skills and utilises another book from the **Dandelion Readers Set 2 Units 11-20** series is available at the end of the chapter.

Planning for Game Day

The Game Plan in Chapter 4 was designed using the same backwards planning approach as Chapters 1–3. Backwards planning ensures the activities in the Structured Literacy routines are aligned with patterns, vocabulary and text pupils will encounter in the accompanying book. The sequence for backwards planning is shared in the breakout box on page 90.

Backwards Planning Using a Decodable Text

Planning Reading Activities (Sentences, Single Words, RAN Charts and Letter Sounds)

Step 1: Choose three sentences from the text. Select sentences that offer practice for target phonics skills.

Step 2: Select four individual words that appear in the sentences for single word reading practice.

Step 3: To build RAN charts, use the four individual words and appropriate short phrases from the sentences.

Step 4: Choose the letters and rime patterns from the single word practice to teach sound-symbol correspondence. In addition, include individual practice with the pronunciation of suffix -s.

Planning Phonemic Awareness Activity

Use the words from the Single Word Reading activity for phonemic awareness (blending).

Planning Heart Word and Dictation Activity

Step 1: Choose up to four heart words from the text.

Step 2: Select rime patterns, one heart word, three single words and at least one sentence from the reading activities for dictation tasks.

Planning Vocabulary and Comprehension Activities

Step 1: Select a word with multiple meanings from the book and develop 'W' questions to elicit pupils' connections or associations with the multiple meanings.

Step 2: Read the text and craft questions that require pupils to find the information in the text (factual questions), analyse word meaning (semantic questions) or "read between the lines" to understand the deeper purpose of the text (inference questions). Set a purpose for reading by asking pupils to keep a particular question in mind as they read the book.

Winning Strategies

The Game Plan for this chapter, Building Stamina with Longer Words, includes the following three Winning Strategies to help pupils in this phase of reading:

- Backwards decoding with initial adjacent consonants and digraphs
- Reading and spelling with suffix -s
- Expanding vocabulary knowledge with multiple-meaning words

Backwards Decoding with Initial Adjacent Consonants and Digraphs

The backwards decoding strategy is introduced in Chapter 2 (pages 43 and 47) with three-letter short vowel words (e.g. sad, sip, mat). It is expanded in Chapter 3 (pages 70 and 72) with four-letter words that contain rime patterns with adjacent consonants (e.g. must, went) and digraphs (e.g. cash, with). The Game Plans in this chapter address the most complex short vowel words, these being four- and five-letter words that include initial adjacent consonants or digraphs and that may also incorporate adjacent consonants or digraphs in the rime pattern (e.g. grass, chips, plank). As words increase in length, additional cognitive demands are placed on the reader in order to sequence sounds correctly. Once words exceed three letters in length, some children struggle with accurate sequencing, and it can negatively impact their reading and/or spelling. For example, some pupils may sound out a word correctly (e.g. /s/ /p/ /l/ /a/ /t/) but mispronounce the whole word when they blend the sounds (e.g. spit). Others may spell the word but omit a letter (e.g. slat). Reinforcing pupils' ability to backwards decode by pronouncing the rime pattern first and practising the adjacent consonants or digraph as an isolated letter chunk supports both automatic word recognition and efficient spelling. For more information about backwards decoding, see Chapters 2 and 3.

Reading and Spelling with Suffix -s

Prefixes and suffixes, collectively known as affixes, play a crucial role in developing word recognition and helping pupils to understand and expand their vocabulary. Pupils' knowledge about morphology not only supports their word recognition but also provides key information about the meaning and function of words in context. Morphology refers to the structure of meaningful word parts. These word parts are called morphemes. Morphemes fall into different categories: base words, prefixes, suffixes and roots. Approximately 60–80 per cent of multisyllabic words pupils encounter beyond the age of eight or so include prefixes and suffixes (Anglin et al, 1993). The addition of prefixes and suffixes increases the length of words. This increased length often acts as a bottleneck to reading achievement. Therefore, practising the automatic recognition of morphemes supports reading fluency and aids with text comprehension. Teaching these word parts equips learners with tools that help them to decode unfamiliar words, enhancing their reading comprehension and writing skills. Understanding how to break down words into meaningful units allows pupils to deduce meaning from context, recognise patterns in word formation and create new words themselves.

In the Game Plans, morphology instruction begins with suffixes. Suffixes are a more commonly occurring morpheme in foundational texts. The word suffix is a combination of the Latin prefix "sub", meaning "after", and the Latin root "fīgere", meaning "to fasten" or "to attach". When combined, "suffix" literally means "to fasten underneath" or "to attach after". This makes sense, as a suffix is attached to the end of a word.

Making Meaning of Morphemes

Morphology is the study of meaningful word parts. Individual word parts that carry meaning are called morphemes. One type of morpheme is an affix. Affixes are letter groups that carry meaning and, when attached to a base or root word, change its job or purpose. There are two categories of affixes, prefixes and suffixes.

- Prefixes are added to the beginning of a root word and modify its meaning (e.g. un- in "unhappy" means "not".)
- Suffixes are added to the end of a root word and often change the word's grammatical category (e.g. -ness in "happiness" turns an adjective into a noun).

Expanding Vocabulary Knowledge with Multiple-Meaning Words

The ability to automatically recognise words is not just based on the letters and sounds. Word recognition also recruits additional aspects of word knowledge. One primary aspect is word meaning. The beauty of Game Plans based on Structured Literacy is the inclusion of all aspects of word knowledge. Vocabulary knowledge refers to both the number of words pupils know and the depth of knowledge about individual words. Significant evidence points to the power of deep vocabulary knowledge as it relates to the speed of retrieval and overall reading fluency and comprehension (Carrier, 2011; Wright & Cervetti, 2017; Zipke et al, 2009). This is especially true for complex words, including those with multiple meanings (polysemous words). Nearly 75 per cent of words children encounter will be polysemous (Zipf, 1945). The more frequent a word, the more likely it is to be polysemous.

Deep Vocabulary Processing Facilitates Comprehension

To use word knowledge for reading fluency and comprehension, pupils must efficiently retrieve a word's meaning and associations. Efficient retrieval is associated with a deep level of knowledge about the target word. When meaning is challenging to retrieve, the reader is forced to expend resources needed for comprehension. Words are more efficiently retrieved when they are robustly represented in the memory.

By incorporating instruction that highlights initial adjacent consonants, the recognition and meaning of foundational suffixes and the multiple meanings of common vocabulary words, educators simultaneously support readers' stamina and comprehension.

Executing Your Game Plan

Step 1: Maximise Phonemic Awareness Instruction

Our ability to recognise, identify and manipulate individual sounds in spoken words is called phonemic awareness. Phonemic awareness activities that have high utility include blending and segmenting. These skills are most closely related to our abilities to decode and encode. In the Game Plan, the words used in the phonemic awareness activities are pulled directly from the text and address the lesson's target phonics skills. If the text offers a limited selection of practice words, bolster your activity with additional words that follow your target pattern. See Chapter 1 (page 24) for **Teacher Script for Introducing, Modelling and Practising Phonemic Awareness**.

Words for Phonemic Awareness Blending Activity in Game Plan

Sounds to Blend	Whole Word
/g/ /r/ /a/ /s/	grass
/p/ /i/ /n/ /ch/	pinch
/s/ /m/ /e/ /l/ /t/	smelt
/b/ /e/ /n/ /ch/	bench
/ch/ /i/ /p/ /s/	chips
/ch/ /i/ /p/	Chip

Step 2: Teach Phonics Concepts Using Winning Strategies

The target phonics skills for the Game Plan include the automatic decoding and spelling of four- and five-letter short vowel words with initial adjacent consonants or digraphs. Select several CCVC and CCVCC words from the decodable text to use for instruction in the Winning Strategies.

WINNING STRATEGY: Backwards Decoding with Initial Adjacent Consonants and Digraphs

As pupils build foundational reading skills, texts begin to increase in complexity. One aspect of text complexity involves the expanding length of individual words in a text. Just as moving from three-sound to four-sound words places additional demands on pupils' auditory memory, words that begin with more than one sound can be difficult, or "sticky", because they place a sequencing burden on the reader. A word's onset, or starter, is composed of either a single consonant (e.g. fit, pump, wish), a digraph (e.g. ship, think, when) or adjacent consonants (e.g. flash, blob, slip). Digraphs are two letters that are pronounced as one sound. There are a limited number of onset digraphs in English, and they include the following: sh, wh, th, ch, ph, kn and wr. Adjacent consonants refer to two or more consonant sounds that are blended together. There are a larger number of adjacent consonants than digraphs, including bl, sl, pl, spl, br, tr, pr, dr, and sp.

Step-by-Step Instruction for Introducing Sticky Starters

Although linguists refer to the initial sound in a word as the onset, pupils are likely more familiar with the term "starter". Sticky Starters are more difficult to manage than regular starters because they contain several letters. Educators are encouraged to introduce pupils to the function of word parts by using child-friendly language. Teachers can introduce Sticky Starters by referencing previous work with single starters and rime patterns. Just as backwards decoding supports the automatic recognition of words with single starters, as discussed in Chapters 2 and 3, the technique will also build efficiency as pupils read words with Sticky Starters. The backwards decoding strategy for Sticky Starter words demonstrates how to break up words into larger chunks. First, pupils are instructed to read the rime pattern, then pronounce the Sticky Starter in isolation. Next, they are prompted to blend the two word parts. Finally, they are instructed to re-pronounce the whole word.

Teacher Script for Introducing and Practising Sticky Starters

Introduction to Strategy

Teacher: *We have been practising reading by rime pattern and adding a single consonant at the start. Today we will practise adding adjacent consonants, which we call Sticky Starters. To be a Sticky Starter, you need at least two consonants that stick close together and blend their sounds.*

Type of Words

Single-Syllable Short Vowel Words with Adjacent Consonants at the Beginning (CCVC and CCVCC Words)

Teacher Language and Prompt for Modelling

Write "ap".

Teacher: *Rime pattern.* (Elicit "-ap".)

Write "cl".

Teacher: *This is our Sticky Starter, "cl-". When I want you to pronounce the Sticky Starter, I will prompt you. Let's practise. Sticky Starter.* (Elicit "cl-".)

Teacher: *Next, we blend the Sticky Starter and rime pattern to say the word. My turn. "Clap". Now your turn. Blend the parts.* (Elicit "clap".) *Finally, we say the whole word again. My turn. "Clap". Your turn.* (Elicit "clap".)

Step 3: Reinforce Letters/Sounds in Isolation

To help pupils build accuracy and automaticity in matching letters to their corresponding sounds, Game Plans include activities for practising consonants, vowels, digraphs, adjacent consonants, rime patterns and affixes in isolation. Teaching familiar letter patterns such as rime units, adjacent consonants and affixes facilitates the recognition of word parts and enables greater automaticity in word recognition and spelling. The Game Plan features the isolated practice of Sticky Starters and rime patterns featured in the text *Chips for Lunch*. See Chapter 1 (page 28) for the **Teacher Script for Introducing, Modelling and Practising Letter/Sound Review** as necessary.

Letter/Sound Review for Game Plan

gr-	sm-	pl-	-ank	-ch	-elt

Connection between Suffixes and Syntax

It is difficult to teach the pronunciation and purpose of word parts without first reviewing what pupils know about syntax and parts of speech. Affixes, particularly suffixes, tend to affect the parts of speech, or the jobs words play, in sentences. Prior to introducing words with suffixes, offer a child-friendly mini-lesson on parts of speech. A mini-lesson provides clarity and ensures all pupils have the same understanding of the "jobs" words have in a sentence. Here you can find a succinct explanation of the parts of speech that can be used in your mini-lesson.

Definitions and Examples of Basic Parts of Speech for a Mini-Lesson

Part of Speech	Definition	Examples from Text
Noun	A word that names a person, place, thing or animal.	Chen, Liz, chips, bench, grass, ants
Verb	A word that names an action.	get, left, smelt, chomp
Adjective	A word that describes a noun.	hot

Step 4: Teach and Practise with Suffixes

One target phonics skill for the Game Plan is the automatic decoding and spelling of short vowel words with suffix -s.

WINNING STRATEGY: Reading and Spelling with Suffix -s

Introducing the pronunciation and purpose of suffixes is often best achieved by utilising pupils' knowledge of oral language. This process entails drawing a comparison between the meaning of an independent base word and the meaning of a base word that has a suffix attached. Instruction commonly begins with suffixes because they are a more common affix in foundational texts.

Step-by-Step Instruction for Introducing Suffix -s

Once pupils understand parts of speech, educators can discuss the purpose of affixes and introduce the first suffix, -s. For example, a teacher might offer the following explanation: "Suffixes are word parts that have the power to change the meaning of the base word. Suffixes are found at the end of the word, and the word 'suffix' comes from the Latin words that mean 'attach after'. Some suffixes change the base word in one way, while other suffixes have the power to change the base word in different ways."

Each subsequent suffix is initially introduced by spelling and pronunciation, and then the meaning or meanings of the suffix are explained. By providing explicit, systematic instruction about affixes, all pupils are offered clarity about the purpose, pronunciation and spelling of these important word parts. For specific teacher language, see the **Teacher Script to Introduce Suffix -s with Nouns** on page 98 and the **Teacher Script to Introduce Suffix -s with Verbs** on page 99.

Wait to Teach the Second Meaning of Suffix -s

It is recommended that you wait at least one day before teaching pupils the other way suffix -s can change the meaning of the base word. Otherwise, pupils might become confused.

Parts of Speech Can Be Tricky

Pupils' understanding of parts of speech will likely evolve as they move through primary school. Multiple-meaning words that can function as both nouns and verbs are often tricky for Year 1 pupils to discern. Mastery in this area is not necessary to continue with instruction in affixes. Educators are encouraged to continue weaving in discussions about parts of speech. Chapter 6 (pages 151–152) provides more depth on breaking up sentences into their phrasing structures with a technique called Syntactic Phrasing.

Teacher Script to Introduce the Suffix -s with Nouns

Introduction to Strategy

Teacher: *Today, I want to introduce you to a word part. These word parts can be attached to base words, and they have the power to change the meaning and pronunciation of the base word. The word parts we will be learning about are called suffixes. "Suffix" is a Latin word that means "attached after". Let me show you how it works.*

Type of Words

Single-Syllable Short Vowel Words with Initial Adjacent Consonants or Digraphs (CCVC or CCVCC Words) + Suffix -s

Introduce Spelling and Pronunciation of Suffix -s

Write -s on the board.

Teacher: *Here is the suffix -s. It is pronounced /s/ and sometimes /z/.* (Elicit correct pronunciation.)

Reading Nouns with Suffix -s

Teacher: *Suffix -s has two jobs. The first job of suffix -s is changing a single noun into a plural noun (i.e. more than one).* (Elicit correct pronunciation.)

Write "chip".

Teacher: *What is our base word?* (Elicit "chip".)

When we see the word "chip", we think of one thing.

Add suffix -s to the base word "chip" to get "chips".

Teacher: *Notice that I attached the suffix -s at the end of the base word. The 's' changes the meaning of the base word to more than one. We no longer imagine one single chip all alone. Now we think of a lot of chips. Let's practise with a few more words.*

Additional Practice

1. plank + s = planks
2. hand + s = hands
3. shop + s = shops

Teacher Script to Introduce the Suffix -s with Verbs

Introduction to Strategy

Teacher: *Today, we will continue our discussion of suffixes. These word parts can be attached to base words, and they have the power to change the meaning and pronunciation of the base word.*

Type of Words

Single-Syllable Short Vowel Words with Initial Adjacent Consonants or Digraphs (CCVC or CCVCC Words) + Suffix -s

Introduce Spelling and Pronunciation of Suffix -s

Write -s on the board.

Teacher: *Here is the suffix -s. It is pronounced /s/ and sometimes /z/.* (Elicit correct pronunciation.)

Teacher: *Let's review the first job of suffix -s.*

Write "chip" and "chips" on the board.

The first job of suffix -s is to make a single noun into a ________. (Elicit "plural".)

Reading Verbs with Suffix -s

Teacher: *The second job of suffix -s is changing a verb into an action that one person is doing right now.*

Write "Chen and Liz rest."

Teacher: *What does our sentence say?* (Elicit "Chen and Liz rest.") *When I read that sentence, I picture two people resting.*

Write "Chen rest."

Teacher: *What does our sentence say?* (Elicit "Chen rest.") *That is an inaccurate sentence. In English, when one person is completing an action right now, we add suffix -s to the verb. Which word is the verb/action?* (Elicit "rest".)

Add the suffix -s to the verb. The sentence should now read "Chen rests."

Teacher: *Now let's practise with a few more. I will write an inaccurate sentence. You name the verb that needs the suffix -s to be accurate.*

Step 5: Apply Phonics Concept to Single Words from the Text

The Game Plan features four words from the text *Chips for Lunch*. Each word includes at least one of the target skills – initial adjacent consonants or digraphs and/or the suffix -s.

Individual Words for Game Plan

grass	plank	smelt	chips

Step-by-Step Instruction for Reading Words with Sticky Starters or Digraphs and Suffix -s

Single word reading instruction, including words with suffixes, always begins by backwards decoding the rime pattern. This approach is an efficient way to read words by chunks and results in greater fluency and accuracy. Pupils should wait to read the suffix until they have fully pronounced the base word. Following this sequence, pupils circle or ignore the suffix and first read the rime pattern. Then, pupils pronounce the Sticky Starter or digraph in isolation, blend the two word parts and re-pronounce the base word. The final step is pronouncing the combined form of the base word and suffix. (See page 101 for **Teacher Script for Backwards Decoding Sticky Starter Words from the Text**.) If it is more appropriate for you to teach words with single starters, you may want to refer back to Chapter 2 for backwards decoding recommendations and script.

WINNING STRATEGY:
Backwards Decoding with Initial Adjacent Consonants or Digraphs and Suffix -s

Ongoing use of the backwards decoding strategy with short vowel words that contain a Sticky Starter, adjacent consonants and/or suffix -s supports the development of automaticity and accuracy with longer words.

Teacher Script for Backwards Decoding Sticky Starter Words from the Text

Introduction to Strategy

Teacher: *We have been practising reading by rime pattern and adding a single consonant at the start. Today we will practise with adjacent consonants, which we call Sticky Starters. To be a Sticky Starter, you need at least two consonants that stick close together and blend their sounds.*

Type of Word

Short Vowel Words with Sticky Starters (CCVC and CCVCC Words)	Short Vowel Words with Sticky Starters or Digraphs and Suffixes

Teacher Language and Prompt for Modelling

Write "elt".

Teacher: *Rime pattern.* (Elicit "-elt".)

Write "sm".

Teacher: *This is our Sticky Starter, "sm-". When I want you to pronounce the Sticky Starter, I will prompt you. Let's practise.*

Sticky Starter. (Elicit "sm-".)

Next, we blend the Sticky Starter and rime pattern to say the word.

My turn. "smelt".

Now your turn. (Elicit "smelt".)

Finally, we say the whole word again.

My turn. "smelt".

Your turn. (Elicit "smelt".)

Write "chips".

Teacher: *This word has a suffix -s. I am going to circle the suffix and save reading it until we have figured out our base word.*

Let's look at the base word. Rime pattern. (Elicit "-ip".)

Sticky Starter. (Elicit "ch-".)

Blend the sounds. (Elicit "chip".)

Repeat the base word. (Elicit "chip".)

Pronounce the suffix. (Elicit "-s".)

Combine the suffix and base word. (Elicit "chips".)

Additional Practice

Example: **champs**

1: Teacher writes "champs".

2: Teacher circles suffix -s.

3: Teacher says "rime pattern"; pupils say "-amp".

4: Teacher says "Sticky Starter"; pupils say "ch-".

5: Teacher says "blend"; pupils say "champ".

6: Teacher says "Repeat the base word"; pupils say "champ".

7: Teacher says "Suffix?"; pupils say "-s".

8: Teacher says "Whole word?"; pupils say "champs".

Differentiating Instruction for Greater Support

There are a few key phonics rules to keep in mind when reading words with Sticky Starters; namely, how to differentiate instruction for pupils who struggle with accurate or automatic blending of the entire Sticky Starter and how to teach digraphs. See **Teacher Script for Differentiating Backwards Decoding with Sticky Starters**.

Differentiating Instruction to Break Up Adjacent Consonants

Differentiating instruction to break up adjacent consonants is appropriate when pupils struggle to accurately produce the initial adjacent consonants. Using the backwards decoding method, educators sequence word reading to activate auditory memory for known words. In order to sequence efficiently, present the rime pattern, then add the consonant closest to the rime pattern and finally blend the initial consonant with the rest of the word. For example, in the word "plank", present "-ank" (rime pattern), then "lank" and finally read "plank". This methodology preserves the form of the word in pupils' auditory memory and allows them to leverage the sequence of sounds for mapping the letter patterns accurately (Kilpatrick, 2020). (See the following **Teacher Script for Differentiating Backwards Decoding with Sticky Starters** for additional guidance.)

Digraph Starters

Digraph starters are never split, because the letters in a digraph are no longer individually discernible; rather, they are coarticulated into one sound.

Teacher Script for Differentiating Backwards Decoding with Sticky Starters

Reading Words with Entire Sticky Starter

Example: stick

1: Teacher writes "ick"; pupils say "-ick".

2: Teacher adds letters "st"; pupils say "st-".

3: Teacher says "blend"; pupils say "stick".

4: Teacher prompts "Whole word?"; pupils say "stick".

Reading Words One Consonant at a Time

Example: stick

1: Teacher writes "ick"; pupils say "-ick".

2: Teacher adds letter "t"; pupils say "tick".

3: Teacher adds letter "s"; pupils say "stick".

4: Teacher prompts "Whole word?"; pupils say "stick".

Step 6: Heart Words

Almost every text contains frequently occurring "tricky" words that break the rules of phonics and are impossible to decode. The Game Plan features four heart words from the story *Chips for Lunch*.

The heart word strategy for learning irregular words capitalises on the idea that each heart word has only one or two irregular spelling features. Rather than instructing a pupil to memorise the whole word, heart word instruction provides a strategy that emphasises segmenting the sounds in the word, producing the phonetically regular spellings for sounds and memorising the one or two irregularly spelt sounds.

Each heart word in the Game Plan for *Chips for Lunch* is divided into sounds in the table titled **Heart Words for Game Plan**. The part of the word that is irregularly spelt is identified with a heart. For scripting on teaching heart words, see Chapter 2 (pages 52–53).

Heart Words for Game Plan

As a teacher, be sure to model breaking the words into sounds and matching letters for each sound. The part of the word indicated by the heart is "irregular" and has to be memorised by heart.

Sound 1	Sound 2
/th/	/u/
th	**e**

Sound 1	Sound 2
/w/	/ir/
w	**ere**

Sound 1	Sound 2	Sound 3
/s/	/e/	/d/
s	**e**	d

Sound 1	Sound 2	Sound 3
/p/	/oo/	/t/
p	**u**	t

Step 7: Enhance Sight Word Recognition with RAN Charts

The Game Plan RAN charts include the individual words and phrases featured in other parts of the lesson. These frequently occurring words, letter patterns and common phrases provide the repetition and practice necessary for some pupils to develop automatic word retrieval skills as they read across a line of text (Wolf et al, 2009). For guidance on teaching a RAN chart and differentiating instruction as needed, refer to Chapter 3 (pages 77–79).

RAN Charts for Game Plan

on the grass	smelt the chips	on the plank	pinch the chips
smelt the chips	on the grass	pinch the chips	on the plank
on the plank	pinch the chips	on the grass	smelt the chips
pinch the chips	smelt the chips	on the plank	on the grass

grass	plank	smelt	chips
plank	grass	chips	smelt
smelt	chips	grass	plank
chips	plank	smelt	grass

Step 8: Practise Reading Sentences from the Text

The Game Plan has selected the following sentences from the text *Chips for Lunch* because they include words that contain Sticky Starters or digraphs (e.g. Chen, chips, grass, smelt, plank) and/or suffix -s (e.g. chips). These phonics concepts are the target skills for the lesson and the selected text offers plenty of opportunity for pupils to apply their word recognition strategies and develop fluency and comprehension.

Sentences for Game Plan

Chen put the chess set on the grass.
Pip and Tess smelt the chips.
Tess and Pip got up on to the plank to pinch the chips from the bag.

Adjusting Sentences to Support Comprehension

As you select your sentences, consider the following:

1. Include sentences in your lesson that offer plentiful opportunities to practise the target skill(s).
2. Select a variety of sentence lengths and styles to support skill generalisation (for example, sentences with and without dialogue).
3. Choose sentences that are simple to comprehend as standalone statements. That may require replacing pronouns with proper nouns (e.g. replace "he" with "Chen").

Step 9: Expand Text-Related Vocabulary Knowledge

The vocabulary activities incorporated into the Game Plan support the development of word recognition skills by deepening pupils' knowledge of multiple-meaning words. Deep vocabulary knowledge enhances reading fluency, speed of retrieval and comprehension. Fluent readers retrieve word meanings quickly and accurately. When retrieval is challenging, it detracts from comprehension. Efficient retrieval is linked to well-established connections between different aspects of word knowledge, including word meanings and associations (Pexman et al, 2008).

Vocabulary Word for Game Plan

Vocabulary Term
plank
Pupil-Friendly Definition 1
A long, thick board. (noun)
Using the Term in a Sentence
The carpenter grabbed the plank of wood from the back of his truck.
Pupil-Friendly Definition 2
An exercise where you support your outstretched, face-down body with your arms and toes. (verb)
Using the Term in a Sentence
The instructor ended the exercise class with a series of planks.
Questions for Discussion

- What does planking look like?
- Why might this exercise move be called a plank?
- What are some things you need a plank of wood for?

WINNING STRATEGY: Expanding Vocabulary Knowledge with Multiple-Meaning Words

The word "plank" is used for vocabulary instruction in the current Game Plan because it is a multiple-meaning word and contains the target phonics patterns. Commonly occurring one-syllable short vowel words are useful for deepening pupils' word associations as they frequently have more than one meaning. See the table **Common Short Vowel Multiple-Meaning Words** on page 107.

Vocabulary knowledge expands through a hierarchy of knowledge development that begins with limited familiarity and develops to comprehensive knowledge (Beck et al, 2013).

Common Short Vowel Multiple-Meaning Words

back	bill	cap	duck	flip	hot	left	pen	sack	tip
bag	bit	check	dust	flop	jig	log	pitch	shed	top
band	blank	cut	fish	fret	kid	mat	pump	sink	track
bank	block	deck	flag	gum	land	mint	quit	slab	trunk
bash	camp	dip	flap	hit	lash	mop	ring	sting	web
bat	can	dish	flat	hog	lap	pack	run	tab	well

Teacher Language and Prompt for Modelling

The mechanism by which pupils develop their levels of vocabulary knowledge is a combination of explicit instruction and active processing (Wright & Cervetti, 2017).

Levels of Vocabulary Knowledge	
Generating Contextual Use	Using the word in a new sentence or text
Receptive Contextual Use	Understanding the word's meaning in a sentence; offering an antonym; correctly identifying examples and non-examples of the vocabulary word
Limited Knowledge	Identifying the basic definition of a vocabulary word

Explicit Instruction

As multiple-meaning vocabulary words are introduced, explicit instruction is characterised by child-friendly definitions and associated sentences, as well as illustrations of meaning.

Active Processing

Active processing of word meanings is accomplished by eliciting pupils' associations with words and asking them to analyse scenarios where the word serves as appropriate terminology. By posing guided questions that probe when, where, who, what and how pupils have experienced the word, educators elicit pupils' associations. The conversational nature of vocabulary instruction lends itself to partner, small group or whole class dialogue, where individual pupils can benefit from the collective experiences of their classmates. For example, since "stick" can mean "adhere", classmates can discuss the various tools available to make objects stick, such as glue and tape. The benefits of sticking paper together instead of stapling or using a paper clip can also be explored. The essential principle is that the more associations pupils can connect to a word, personal or relational, the greater their automaticity when retrieving its meanings and roles in text (Pexman et al, 2008).

Step 10: Putting It All Together for Text Reading and Comprehension

Ultimately, building word recognition skills is a pathway to ensuring fluent reading and comprehension. Although decodable texts are short and often limited in content, the passages still present opportunities to practise multiple aspects of pupils' comprehension, including factual, inferential and vocabulary knowledge.

A series of comprehension questions have been developed to assess different aspects of pupils' understanding. (For guidance on whole group, choral or partner reading and strategies teachers can employ to activate background knowledge and set a purpose for reading, see Chapters 2 and 3.)

Comprehension Questions for Game Plan

Factual
Why did Chen leave the chips on the bench?

Inferential
How do Pip and Tess get to the chips?

Vocabulary in Context
How do you think Chen and Liz feel at the end of the story?

Text from the Book *Chips for Lunch*
Chen and Liz went to get chips for lunch. The chips were hot. Chen left the chips on the bench.
"Let's get the chess set," said Liz. "I am a champ at chess." Chen put the chess set on the grass.
Pip and Tess smelt the chips. "Let's pinch the chips," said Pip. Pip got a plank and set it up.
Tess and Pip got up on to the plank to pinch the chips from the bag. Bad ants!
The bugs sat on the grass. "Let's chomp on the chips," said Pip. Yum! Yum!
Chen and Liz got up and sat on the bench. "Just six chips left! The ants got the chips!" yelled Chen.

Step 11: Applying Phonics Knowledge to Dictation

A selection of words and sentences from the text *Chips for Lunch* have been used to plan the dictation routine. Dictation serves as an additional learning opportunity to solidify skills through instruction, rather than serving as an assessment. Suggested language for completing the dictation exercise can be found in Chapter 2 (pages 60–61). If your phonics curriculum has a dictation routine, feel free to utilise those resources in that portion of the routine.

Dictation Routine for Game Plan

Dictation	Selected Elements
Heart Word	put
Letters/Sounds/ Rime Patterns	gr-, pl-, sm-
Words	grass, plank, chips
Sentence	Pip and Tess smelt the chips.

Proposed Practice Schedule

The practice schedule below suggests one method of arranging the activities into approximately 20-minute lessons over the course of three days. Please note that the first day of the lesson does not include connected text, which is a high-leverage activity for building fluency, and we recommend rereading previously learnt sentences for a quick lesson warm-up.

Day 1 (18 mins)	Day 2 (23 mins)	Day 3 (20 mins)
Phonics (5 mins)	Heart Words (5 mins)	RAN Chart – Phrases (5 mins)
Letter Sounds (3 mins)	Sentences (5 mins)	Dictation (10 mins)
Single Words (5 mins)	Vocabulary (8 mins)	Finish Book/Read Another Book (5 mins)
RAN Chart – Single Words (5 mins)	Book Reading (5 mins)	

Game Plan

Decodable Text: ***The Cash*, Dandelion Readers Set 2 Units 11-20, Book 12**
Phonics Concept: **Recognition of short vowel words with initial adjacent consonants or digraphs (CCVC and CCVCC); suffix -s**

Phonemic Awareness			**Phonics Concept**
stop	spend	spent	Provide direct instruction in the phonics concept, utilising words pulled from the Reader and/or that fit the patterns you are teaching.
shelf	cash	best	

Letter/Sound/Rime Review

-op	-end	-ent	-elf	-ash	-am

Suffix Review

-s

Single Word Reading

shelf	spends	spent	shop

Heart Words

to	says	you	has

RAN Charts (Single Words and Phrases)

shelf	spends	spent	shop	at the best shop	from the shelf	spends the cash	Sam stops
shop	shelf	spends	spent	Sam stops	at the best shop	from the shelf	spends the cash
spent	shop	shelf	spends	spends the cash	Sam stops	at the best shop	from the shelf
spends	spent	shop	shelf	from the shelf	spends the cash	Sam stops	at the best shop

Sentence Reading

Sam stops at the best shop.

Sam gets red gum from the shelf and spends the cash.

"But we spent the cash," says Tam.

Multiple-Meaning Word: spend

Definition 1 (v) Paying money for things you want or need.	**Definition 2** (v) Using your time or energy to do something.	**Questions** What are some things that you spend money on? What are some things you spend your time doing?
Sentence 1 During the holiday season, people spend a lot of money.	**Sentence 2** This weekend, I plan to spend some time reorganising my bedroom.	

Story and Comprehension Questions

Why does Mum give Tam and Sam a list?	Why can't Tam and Sam get the items on Mum's list?	One of the items on the shopping list is jam. What does "jam" mean here? How might another meaning of "jam" describe the children's situation?

Dictation

Heart Word	to
Letters/Sounds/Rime Patterns	-op, -ent, -elf
Words	shop, spends, shelf
Sentence	Sam gets gum from the shelf.

Chapter 5

Decoding Multisyllabic Words

- Syllable division for multisyllabic short vowel words
- Spelling rules for words with suffix -s and -es
- Backwards decoding multisyllabic short vowel words
- Spelling rules for multisyllabic short vowel words

Game Plan

Decodable Text: ***The Sandpit*, Dandelion Launchers Units 16-20, Book 17a**
Phonics Concept: **Reading and spelling multisyllabic words with short vowel syllables; syllable division; suffix -s/-es**

Letter/Sound/Rime Review

-ish	-atch	-oth
-ick	-and	-um

Phonics Concept

Provide direct instruction in the phonics concept, utilising words pulled from the Reader and/or that fit the patterns you are teaching.

Suffix Review

-s	-es

Single Word Reading

dishcloth	picnic	drumstick	sandwich

Heart Words

island	have	give	says

RAN Charts (Single Words and Phrases)

picnic	dishcloth	sandwich	drumstick	has a dishcloth	grabs her lunchbox	Meg snatches	the drumstick
picnic	sandwich	drumstick	dishcloth	grabs her lunchbox	has a dishcloth	the drumstick	Meg snatches
sandwich	drumstick	dishcloth	picnic	Meg snatches	the drumstick	has a dishcloth	grabs her lunchbox
dishcloth	picnic	drumstick	sandwich	the drumstick	grabs her lunchbox	Meg snatches	has a dishcloth

Sentence Reading

Viv has a dishcloth with a skull on it.

"Let's have a picnic on the island," says Viv and grabs her lunchbox.

Just then, Meg snatches the drumstick!

Multiple-Meaning Word: drumstick

Definition 1 (n) The lower part of the leg of a chicken, which is cooked and eaten.	**Definition 2** (n) Sticks used for making music on a drum.	**Questions** When might someone eat a drumstick? What type of musician might use drumsticks? How does it sound when drumsticks hit a drum?
Sentence 1 We will have drumsticks and mashed potatoes for dinner tonight.	**Sentence 2** My brother got new drumsticks in music class.	

Story and Comprehension Questions

What are Fred and Viv doing in the sandpit?	Why does Meg run off with the drumstick?	What does the word "bandit" mean?

Dictation

Heart Word	island
Letters/Sounds/Rime Patterns	-ish, -atch, -oth
Words	dishcloth, picnic, drumstick
Sentence	Meg snatches the drumstick.

In practice, RAN phrases should be displayed across a single line.

Target Skills for Game Plan

As pupils encounter increasingly sophisticated text, they will need guidance in reading a broader range of words, including multisyllabic words and those with suffixes. Effective teaching and recognition of multisyllabic words combines strategic instruction with purposeful practice opportunities. Instruction is characterised by strategies that break down longer words into efficient chunks and the integration of practice opportunities that support the application of skills to text. Additional activities offer guidance with spelling rules, connections to word meaning and support for reading comprehension. Along these lines, the activities and instruction in the Game Plan are designed to develop the following two skills:

- Decoding and spelling multisyllabic words with short vowel sounds
- Spelling with suffix -es

Together, these instructional elements not only support pupils' accuracy in reading longer words but also build their automaticity, fluency and comprehension.

Your Team

Pupils are ready for this lesson when they are able to automatically recognise one-syllable short vowel words with initial adjacent consonants. Word length might range between four and six letters (e.g. span, sprint). Typically, pupils achieve this towards the middle to end of Reception. However, pupils in any phase or year group will benefit from explicit instruction and guided practice if they continue to read words sound by sound or if they generally struggle with reading fluency.

Case Study

Geoff, eight years old, continues to struggle with accurately reading long words in text. When he encounters a long word, he tends to guess based on the context of the text or even the first letter of the word. Geoff has significant background knowledge and often selects texts on topics that are familiar to him. Until recently, Geoff has been able to use his language skills and background knowledge as compensatory strategies. However, the new unit in science requires Geoff to read about a topic that is new to him, and he has struggled to understand the text and answer questions accurately. What strategies can help Geoff become accurate in both reading and spelling multisyllabic words?

Your Equipment

Series: Dandelion Launchers Units 16-20
(ISBN 9781783693337)
Reader: *The Sandpit*
(Book 17a)
Phonics Concept:
Reading and spelling multisyllabic words with short vowel syllables; syllable division; suffix -s/-es.
Book Overview:
Friends enjoy an imaginary quest until their adventure is interrupted by a hungry puppy.

Text from the Book *The Sandpit*

Viv and Fred are in the sandpit.
"Let's pretend this is an island," says Viv.

Fred is a frogman. Viv has a dishcloth with a skull on it.

"Let's have a picnic on the island," says Viv and grabs her lunchbox.

Viv has a sandwich and a plum. Fred has chicken drumsticks.

"I'll give you a chicken leg for that plum."
Fred hands Viv the chicken leg.

Just then, Meg snatches the drumstick!
"Bandit!" yells Viv as Meg runs off.

Additional Texts

An additional Game Plan that targets similar skills and utilises another book from the **Dandelion Launchers Units 16-20** series is available at the end of the chapter.

Planning for Game Day

The Game Plan in Chapter 5 was designed using the same backwards planning approach as Chapters 1–4. Backwards planning ensures the activities in the Structured Literacy routines are aligned with patterns, vocabulary and text pupils will encounter in the accompanying book. The sequence for backwards planning is shared in the breakout box **Backwards Planning Using a Decodable Text** on page 116. Note that the current Game Plan no longer includes phonemic awareness activities. The focus on lesson activities has now shifted to advanced decoding and word recognition. If your pupils require ongoing support in phonemic awareness skill building, refer to the guidance from Chapter 4 for aligning activities that involve "blending" sounds with the words and letter patterns encountered in the accompanying decodable text *The Sandpit*.

Backwards Planning Using a Decodable Text

Planning Reading Activities (Sentences, Single Words, RAN Charts, Letter Sounds and Suffixes)

Step 1: Choose three sentences from the text. Select sentences that offer practice for target phonics skills.

Step 2: Select four individual words that appear in the sentences for single word reading practice.

Step 3: To build RAN charts, use the four individual words and appropriate short phrases from the sentences.

Step 4: Choose the letters and rime patterns from the single word practice to teach sound-symbol correspondence. In addition, include individual practice with the pronunciation of suffix -s and -es.

Planning Heart Word and Dictation Activity

Step 1: Choose up to four heart words from the text.

Step 2: Select rime patterns, one heart word, three single words and at least one sentence from the reading activities for dictation tasks.

Planning Vocabulary and Comprehension Activities

Step 1: Select a multiple-meaning word from the book and develop 'w' questions to elicit pupils' connection or associations with the multiple meanings.

Step 2: Read the story and craft questions that require pupils to find the information in the text (factual questions), analyse word meaning (semantic questions) or "read between the lines" to understand the deeper purpose of the story (inference questions). Set a purpose for reading by providing a question for pupils to keep in mind as they read the book.

Winning Strategies

The instructional routines in the Game Plan support developing pupils' reading and spelling of multisyllabic words and those with the suffix -s or -es through four Winning Strategies:

- Syllable division for multisyllabic short vowel words
- Spelling rules for words with suffix -s and -es
- Backwards decoding multisyllabic short vowel words
- Spelling rules for multisyllabic short vowel words

Syllable Division for Multisyllabic Short Vowel Words

Learning to read in English can be challenging because of the varied pronunciation of vowel sounds. The pronunciation of a vowel is determined by a word's syllable type (for more information about syllables, see the breakout box **Syllable Spotlight**). Once accurate pronunciation of a vowel sound in single-syllable words has been mastered, pupils are ready to move on to multi-syllable words.

Using a strategic approach to read multisyllabic words is critical for overall reading achievement. These are the skills that will serve pupils as they encounter new information. Many pupils become stuck at the single-syllable level, and rather than strategically sounding out longer words, they rely on compensatory strategies for guessing unknown words. The most common compensatory strategies involve guessing, either based on the first letter of the word, the overall appearance of the word or the context in which the word is used (Kilpatrick, 2020). Most multisyllabic words can be decoded utilising a few key syllable division strategies. These approaches break up the word into small units of letter patterns. Teaching and practising syllable division methods ensures that pupils have a strategic approach as they encounter longer and/or unknown words.

Syllable Spotlight

A syllable is a word or part of a word with one vowel sound. Every word in English is made up of at least one syllable. Determining the syllables in a word involves counting the number of vowel sounds, not the number of letters. For example, the word "read" is one syllable because the letters 'ea' only make one vowel sound, /ee/. Other single-syllable words include "soup", "bait" and "flout".

Spelling Rules for Words with Suffix -s and -es

English texts are full of words that contain prefixes and suffixes. Morphologically complex words make up more than half of the words in English. Approximately 60–80 per cent of written words that pupils from the age of nine onwards use have multiple morphemes, including roots, prefixes and suffixes (Anglin et al, 1993). Words with affixes are complex because they are both longer and often contain an additional syllable, or vowel sound, compared to the independent base word. For example, most nouns are made plural by adding one of two suffixes. Suffix -s is added to most words that end with either a consonant or a silent 'e'. When suffix -s is added, the number of syllables in the base word does not change (e.g. cat/cats; lake/lakes). In contrast, suffix -es also creates a plural form of the word, but in the process adds an additional syllable (e.g. crutch/crutches; flash/flashes). Suffix -es is used when words end with 's', 'x', 'z', 'sh' or 'ch' because they "hiss" at the end. When a word ends in a sound that hisses, the vowel 'e' is added to help with the clarity of pronunciation and ensure the plural suffix is clearly processed (Eide, 2012). The complexity of these rules necessitates explicit instruction for most pupils, certainly in spelling, if not reading, which serves as one of the Winning Strategies for the current Game Plan.

Backwards Decoding Multisyllabic Short Vowel Words

Research on word recognition implies that when proficient readers encounter longer, multisyllabic words, they sound them out by chunks. For example, one study that examined efficient strategies for reading multisyllabic words divided pupils into two groups. Group 1 was presented with multisyllabic words one letter at a time. Each letter was in its correct position but flashed only briefly on the screen before the next letter appeared (e.g. f-a-n-t-a-s-t-i-c; t-r-u-m-p-e-t; d-i-s-g-u-s-t). The researchers calculated the amount of time required for participants to name the word they had just viewed. Generally, participants were able to correctly name the word, but only if the interval between the letter presentation was very short. When the interval exceeded even a few seconds, accurate reading became more elusive. In Group 2, the multisyllabic words were divided into syllable chunks, and the word was flashed on the screen one chunk at a time (e.g. fan-tas-tic, trum-pet, dis-gust). The participants in the second group could read the words with greater accuracy than the first group, even when the intervals between syllables was lengthened by several seconds (Mewhort & Beal, 1977). The implications of these findings lay the groundwork for our syllable instruction, which guides readers not only to divide syllables but also to sound them out from the back to the front, thereby activating our auditory memory for common word chunks.

Number of Syllables	Example Words Divided by Syllable with Underlined Vowel Sound
1	I, bed, split, cone, place, corn, read, soup.
2	pi·lot, hot·dog, or·der, can·not, ba·by
3	per·sis·tent, a·ban·don, com·plic·ate
4	wa·ter·mel·on, es·tab·lish·ment, ac·a·dem·ic

Spelling Rules for Multisyllabic Short Vowel Words

Spelling is particularly challenging for many pupils because it requires the integration of several related skills, including phonemic awareness, phonics, handwriting and memorisation of irregular letter patterns. As words increase in length, spelling complexity increases. The current Game Plan introduces a consistent, multisensory routine that identifies the syllables, segments each sound in an individual syllable and represents them with letters and supports independence and achievement in spelling.

Executing Your Game Plan

Step 1: Teach Phonics Concepts Using Winning Strategies

There are two target phonics skills for the Game Plan. The first target phonics skill is decoding and spelling multisyllabic words with short vowel sounds. The decoding strategy is discussed below, and the spelling strategy for spelling multisyllabic words is introduced in the dictation section of the Game Plan.

WINNING STRATEGY: Syllable Division for Multisyllabic Short Vowel Words

One foundational component of phonics instruction involves the ability to identify, read and spell the syllables found in most English words. Most single-syllable words are straightforward, with one vowel producing one sound (e.g. bed, split). Some single-syllable words have multiple vowels (e.g. read, soup) or R-controlled vowels producing one sound (e.g. corn, thwart). There are six syllable types in English, and each type of syllable shifts the vowel pronunciation (see **The Six Syllable Types in English** on page 120). Some syllable types in English are very common, while others are more rare. The most common syllable type is a closed syllable where the vowel sound is short (e.g. bed, spill, trap, block). Closed syllables can be found in slightly over 40 per cent of English words (Stanback, 1992). Familiarity with common closed syllables, particularly in longer multisyllabic words (e.g. can·not, es·tab·lish·ment), offers pupils a broadly generalisable strategy in the early phases of their reading development.

Introducing a Syllable

Instruction on decoding multisyllabic words begins with a clear and concise definition of a syllable and practice identifying and pronouncing the vowel sound. Syllables can be defined as words or parts of words with one vowel sound. Placing a dot under each letter that represents a vowel sound is an efficient method for visually representing the number of syllables in a word. However, in order to pronounce the vowel sound correctly, it is helpful to underline the rime pattern in the syllable. (See **Identifying Vowel Sound and Rime Pattern in Syllables** on page 120.) Additionally, reading by rime pattern offers a more efficient word recognition strategy compared to sound-by-sound decoding, as described in Chapter 2.

The Six Syllable Types in English

Syllable Type	Vowel Sound	Sample Single-Syllable Words	Sample Multi-Syllable Words
Closed	The vowel sound is short and closed in by consonant sounds.	mad, bed, cot	blank·et, tab·let, cot·ton
Open	The vowel sound is long and is not followed by a consonant.	do, she, go, be	cra·zy, u·nit, fo·cus
R-Controlled	The vowel sound is distorted by the letter 'r' that immediately follows.	corn, tart, bird, surf, her	cor·ner, car·pet, dir·ty
Vowel Digraph	In a vowel digraph, the two vowels work together to represent a sound (e.g. bread, oat, boy, sour).	Vowel Digraph: float, bean, plain, moist	Au·gust, oat·meal, don·key
Split Vowel Spelling	The vowel sound is long and followed by a consonant and split vowel spelling.	blame, Pete, chute, pose	sun·shine, pan·cake, side·walk
Consonant 'le'	This syllable type occurs at the end of words and has a consonant followed by an 'l' and silent 'e'.	N/A	sim·ple, tur·tle, i·ci·cle

(Stanback, 1992)

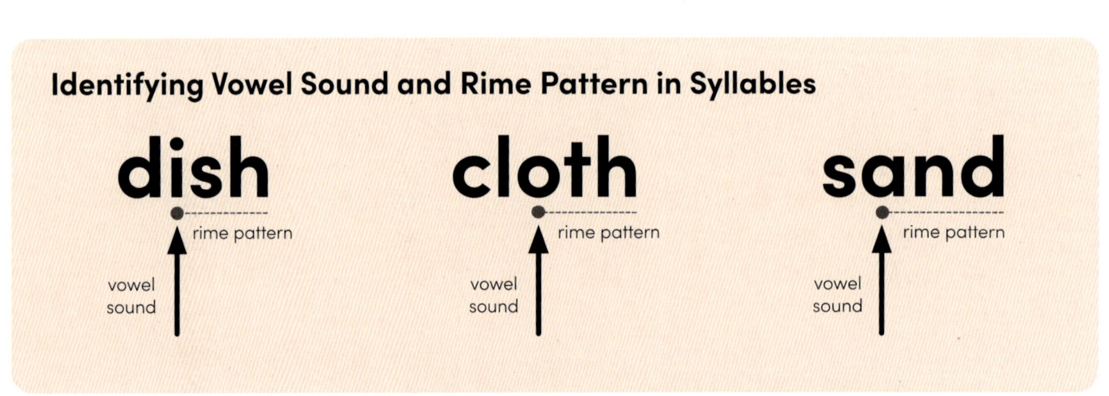

Teacher Script to Introduce Syllables and Practise with Single-Syllable Words

Introduction to Strategy

Teacher: *All words are made up of syllables. Syllables are words or parts of words with one vowel sound. If you have one vowel sound in a word, you have one syllable. If you have two vowel sounds in a word, you have two syllables. If you have three vowel sounds in a word, you have* _____ (elicit "three") *syllables. Let's look at our list of words, find the vowel sounds and count the syllables.*

Type of Word

Single-Syllable Short Vowel Words with Initial/Final Adjacent Consonants or Digraphs (CVCC, CVCCC, CCVC or CCVCC Words)

Counting the Syllables by Finding the Vowel Sound

Write "dish" on the board.

Teacher: *I'm going to run my finger under the word. Put your hand in the air when I reach a letter that makes a vowel sound.* (Stop at letter 'i'.) *We have found our vowel sound. The letter 'i' makes the sound /i/. I'm going to put a dot under the letter making a vowel sound.* (Dot under 'i'.)

Teacher: *The dot will help us find our vowel sound and count our syllables. Are there any other letters that have a vowel sound in this word?* (Elicit "no".) *I am going to look for the dots to count the vowel sounds.* (Count one dot.) *We have one vowel sound, so this must be a one-syllable word.*

Identifying the Rime Pattern for Syllable Pronunciation

Teacher: *Even though we are discussing syllables, I don't want to forget about our rime patterns. Remember rime patterns are the groups of letters in a syllable that start with the vowel. Our vowel 'i' also starts our rime pattern "-ish".*

Teacher: *I'm going to underline the rime pattern.* (Underline "ish".)
Let's read the rime pattern. (Elicit "-ish".)
Now the whole word. (Elicit "dish".)
Now let's practise with a few more.

Dividing Multisyllabic Words

In order to accurately read multisyllabic words, pupils can follow a set of sequential strategies. First, find and dot the letter(s) representing vowel sounds. Second, identify and underline common rime patterns. Next, divide the syllables after the rime pattern. (See **Dot, Underline, and Divide between the Syllables**.)

1. *Dot the letters making vowel sounds.* Pupils dot under each letter making a vowel sound.
2. *Underline the rime pattern.* Find and underline the common rime patterns. In closed syllables where the vowel sound is short, rime patterns are composed of one vowel letter and one or two consonant letters (e.g. -VC as in "-ic" or -VCC as in "-ish").
3. *Divide the syllables.* Multisyllabic closed-syllable words are divided after the rime patterns. If there are double letters, divide the syllable between the letters (e.g. rab·bit).
4. *Read the syllables.* Once the word is accurately divided, correctly pronouncing the syllables involves retrieving the correct vowel sound and blending all the sounds in the correct sequence.
5. *Reread the whole word.* The final step is rereading the whole word as one unit.

Dot, Underline and Divide between the Syllables

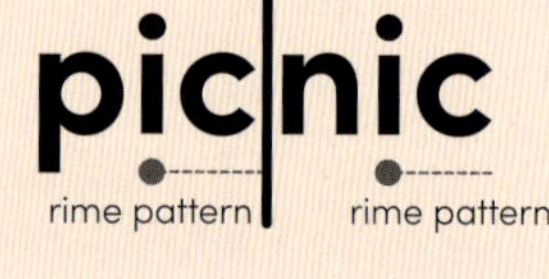

Step 2: Reinforce Letters/Sounds in Isolation

The Game Plan includes activities for practising rime patterns and affixes in isolation. Teaching familiar letter patterns such as rime units and affixes facilitates the recognition of word parts and enables greater automaticity in word recognition and spelling. The Game Plan features six rime patterns and two suffixes featured in the story *The Sandpit*. The focus on rime patterns is intended to ensure that pupils are not only accurate with vowel sound pronunciation but can also blend the vowels with consonant sounds that are common in syllable chunks.

Rime Patterns for Game Plan

-ish	-atch	-oth
-ick	-and	-um

Suffixes for Game Plan

Step 3: Teach and Review Suffixes

WINNING STRATEGY:
Spelling Rules for Words with Suffix -s and -es

Both suffix -s and -es are included in the text *The Sandpit*, and providing pupils with guidance on the similarities, differences and spelling rules for using these suffixes is essential.

Determining when to use -s or -es as a suffix is dependent on the final sounds in the base word. As a reminder, both suffixes -s and -es can change the meaning of a base word in two ways. First, they can make singular nouns plural nouns (e.g. cat/cats; match/matches). Second, verbs are transformed into present tense for a singular subject (e.g. flip/He flips; fish/She fishes).

Teacher Script for Introducing, Modelling and Practising Spelling Words with Suffix -s and -es

Introduction to Strategy

Teacher: *Today we will talk about the two suffixes that can make a word plural.*

Review the Job of Suffix -s

Replicate the table below that identifies the two jobs of suffix -s and examples.

Teacher: *We have already learnt that suffix -s has two jobs. The first job is that it makes a noun plural.*

Teacher: *The second job of suffix -s is to create a present tense verb for a sentence about a single subject (other than you or I).*

-s	
Makes a noun plural	**Creates a present tense verb for a sentence about a single subject**
dog**s** snack**s** bell**s**	He jump**s**. The frog hop**s**.

Describe the Job of Suffix -es

Teacher: *Suffix -es performs the same job as suffix -s. Suffix -es also makes a noun plural.*

Teacher: *The second job of suffix -es is to create a present tense verb for a sentence about a single subject (other than you or I).*

-s	-es
Makes a noun plural	
dog**s**	patch**es**
snack**s**	wish**es**
bell**s**	matchbox**es**

-s	-es
Creates a present tense verb for a sentence about a single subject	
He jump**s**.	She push**es**.
The frog hop**s**.	The cat hiss**es**.

Determine When to Use Suffix -es

Teacher: *When we add the suffix -es, it gives our base word an additional syllable. Let's practise by saying the base word in isolation and then saying it with the suffix -es.* (Model the chin drop method to count syllables as you pronounce each word.) *Say the word "patch" with me – how many syllables?* (Elicit "one".) *Now say "patches". How many syllables?* (Elicit "two".) *The suffix -es is adding a syllable.* (Practise with "push/pushes"; "hiss/hisses".)

Teacher: *It's important to have an extra syllable because some base words end with letters that make a "hissing sound". For example, "push", "wish", "box" and "hiss". It is hard to hear the suffix -s when the base word already hisses. So, we add a suffix with an extra syllable.*

Final Rule

Teacher: *So, our rule is when we hear a base word that ends with a hissing sound, we will add suffix -es. Final letters that make a hissing sound are 's', 'x', 'z', 'sh' or 'ch'.*

Rule for Using -es
Use -es when the base word ends with "hissing" letters.
s (glas**s**es)
x (fo**x**es)
z (buz**z**es)
sh (di**sh**es)
ch (cat**ch**es)

Step 4: Apply Phonics Concept to Single Words from the Text

The keywords in your lesson are featured in the story. They likely make an appearance in the sentence activities and will serve as a platform for practising target phonics and morphology skills. The current Game Plan features four words from the text *The Sandpit*. Each word is relevant to the target reading skill – decoding multisyllabic words.

Individual Words for Game Plan

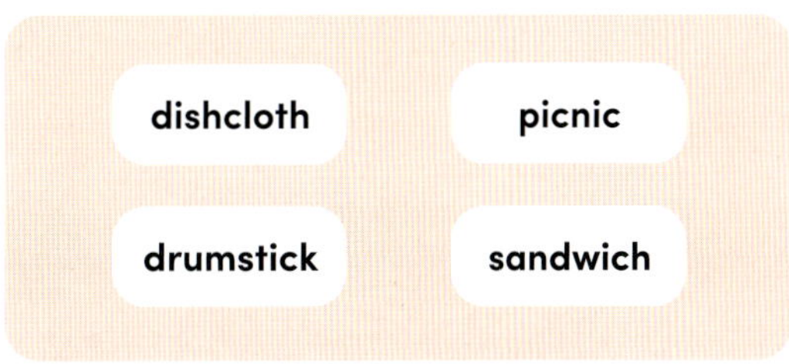

WINNING STRATEGY: Backwards Decoding Multisyllabic Short Vowel Words

Some pupils are able to divide syllables but are challenged by accurate word reading. In certain cases, pupils may struggle to read individual syllables. Others might sound out each syllable correctly but inaccurately pronounce the whole word. This is when backwards decoding is helpful. Instruct pupils to divide the syllables for each word and backwards decode as necessary.

Teacher Script for Backwards Decoding Multisyllabic Words from the Text

Introduction to Strategy

Teacher: *Let's continue breaking up our words by syllable. Then, I want to show you a secret strategy that helps our brain read longer words.*

Type of Words

Two-Syllable Words with Closed Syllables

Syllable Division

Write the first word: "dishcloth".

Teacher: *First, I will find the letters making vowel sounds and put dots underneath.* (Run finger under the word. Put dots under 'i' and 'o'.) *We have found two vowel sounds* (indicate dots), *so we know this is a two-syllable word.*

Teacher: *The dot also indicates where our rime pattern begins. Let's underline our rime patterns.* (Underline the following patterns: d**ish**cl**oth**.) *Now we are ready to divide our word into individual syllables. We will divide after our rime patterns.* (Divide as follows: d**ish**·cl**oth**.)

Backwards Decoding

Teacher: *Let's read the word from the back to the front. That way, we'll warm up our brain for words that have a similar ending pattern.* (Cover all but the last rime pattern.)

Teacher: *"-oth".* (Uncover the remaining starter adjacent consonants "cl".) *"cloth". The final syllable in the word is "cloth", so now our brain is activating all the words we know that have "cloth" at the end. But we aren't going to guess. We will still read the first syllable.* (Uncover the rime pattern in the first syllable and blend with the final syllable.)

Teacher: *"-ish·cloth".* (Uncover the initial sound in the first syllable and blend with remaining parts of the word.) *"dish·cloth". What is the whole word?* (Elicit "dishcloth".)

Step 5: Build Knowledge of Heart Words

Heart Words for Game Plan

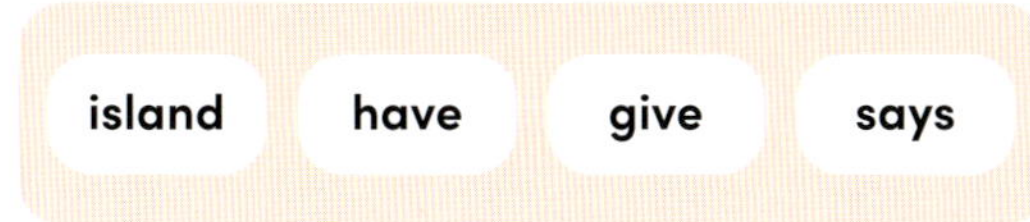

Two-Syllable Heart Words

The **Teacher Script for Modelling and Practising Reading and Writing Heart Words** is introduced in Chapter 2 (pages 52–53). Spelling two-syllable heart words is slightly different because pupils need to divide the word into syllables before segmenting each sound. For example, the heart word "island" is segmented into syllables using an auditory syllabification strategy such as "chin drop", where the hand is placed underneath the chin and you count each time the chin drops while pronouncing a word. The number of times the chin drops corresponds to the number of syllables in the word (e.g. is·land). Then, each syllable is segmented into individual sounds, the letters representing each sound are discussed and the irregular spelling is highlighted using the same method as a single-syllable word. Repeat the procedure for additional words using the same prompts. As a teacher, be sure to model breaking the words into sounds and matching letters for each sound. The part of the word that is highlighted is "irregular" and has to be memorised by heart.

Chin Drop Strategy for Oral Syllable Division

The chin drop strategy is a multisensory technique that helps pupils count the number of syllables in a word. Pupils should be instructed to put their hand under their chin, palm facing down, and pronounce the word. As each vowel is pronounced, they will feel their chin drop, indicating the presence of a new syllable. Pupils count the number of times their chin drops to determine the number of syllables in a word.

Script for Modelling and Practising Reading and Writing Multisyllabic Heart Words

Introduction to Strategy

Teacher: *We have been using the Heart Word Magic approach to learn how to spell and read one-syllable heart words. Now we are going to apply the same strategy to two-syllable words.*

Teacher Language and Prompt for Modelling

Teacher: *The heart word today is "island".*

Write the word on the board and use it in a sentence.

Teacher: *Say "island".*

Pupils repeat the word.

Teacher: *"Island" is spelt i-s-l-a-n-d.* (Spell out the word.)

Pupils write the word on their card.

Teacher: *"Island" is a word with more than one syllable. Let's count the number of times our chin drops when we say "island".*

Pronounce the word slowly and count the number of drops during articulation – two.

Teacher: *Two drops means two syllables. "Island" is a two-syllable word. Let's draw a slash to show there will be two syllables.*

/

Teacher: *The first syllable is /ie/ – one sound* (write one dash) *– and is spelt 'is'. This is the tricky part of the word, and we need to memorise it by heart. So, we will place a heart underneath.*

Teacher: *The second syllable is "land" – four sounds (/l/ /a/ /n/ /d/).*

Write three dashes.

Teacher: */l/ is spelt with 'l'*
/a/ is spelt with 'a'
/n/ is spelt with 'n'
/d/ is spelt with 'd'
All the letters are following the rules you already know, so we don't need a heart.

is / l a n d

Teacher: *Let's read the heart word one more time.* (Pupils run their finger under the word as they read it.)

Teacher: *What was the tricky part in "island"?*

Pupils respond. Pupils add the index card to a card ring for later practice.

Step 6: Enhance Sight Word Recognition with RAN Charts

The Game Plan RAN charts include the individual words and phrases featured in other parts of the lesson. RAN charts are a Winning Strategy from Chapter 3 and are used to practise the automatic retrieval of common single words and phrases and support tracking across a page and the "return sweep" to the next line.

RAN Charts for Game Plan

has a dishcloth	grabs her lunchbox	Meg snatches	the drumstick
grabs her lunchbox	has a dishcloth	the drumstick	Meg snatches
Meg snatches	the drumstick	has a dishcloth	grabs her lunchbox
the drumstick	grabs her lunchbox	Meg snatches	has a dishcloth

picnic	dishcloth	sandwich	drumstick
picnic	sandwich	drumstick	dishcloth
sandwich	drumstick	dishcloth	picnic
dishcloth	picnic	drumstick	sandwich

Step 7: Practise Reading Sentences from the Text

The Game Plan has selected the following sentences from text *The Sandpit* because they include multisyllabic words (e.g. dishcloth, picnic, lunchbox, drumstick) and/or suffix -s/-es (e.g. grabs, snatches). During the Sentence Reading activity, educators can coach pupils to read the sentences silently, and then chorally aloud.

Sentences for Game Plan

Viv has a dishcloth with a skull on it.
"Let's have a picnic on the island," says Viv and grabs her lunchbox.
Just then, Meg snatches the drumstick!

Step 8: Expand Text-Related Vocabulary Knowledge

Activating pupils' knowledge of multiple-meaning words from the text supports the development of their word recognition skills. The word "drumstick" is the multiple-meaning word used in the Game Plan to deepen pupils' vocabulary knowledge and enhance their associations.

Vocabulary Word for Game Plan

Vocabulary Term
drumstick
Pupil-Friendly Definition 1
The lower part of the leg of a chicken, which is cooked and eaten. (noun)
Using the Term in a Sentence
We will have drumsticks and mashed potatoes for dinner tonight.
Pupil-Friendly Definition 2
Sticks used for making music on a drum. (noun)
Using the Term in a Sentence
My brother got new drumsticks in music class.
Questions for Discussion

- When might someone eat a drumstick?
- What type of musician might use drumsticks?
- How does it sound when drumsticks hit a drum?

Step 9: Putting It All Together for Text Reading and Comprehension

Building word recognition skills is a pathway to ensuring fluent reading and comprehension. Although decodable texts are short and often limited in content, the stories or texts still present opportunities to practise multiple aspects of pupils' comprehension, including factual, inferential and vocabulary knowledge. The following questions on page 131 have been generated for the Game Plan.

Comprehension Questions for Game Plan

Factual
What are Fred and Viv doing in the sandpit?

Inferential
Why does Meg run off with the drumstick?

Vocabulary in Context
What does the word "bandit" mean?

Text from the Book *The Sandpit*

Viv and Fred are in the sandpit. "Let's pretend this is an island," says Viv.

Fred is a frogman. Viv has a dishcloth with a skull on it.

"Let's have a picnic on the island," says Viv and grabs her lunchbox.

Viv has a sandwich and a plum. Fred has chicken drumsticks.

"I'll give you a chicken leg for that plum." Fred hands Viv the chicken leg.

Just then, Meg snatches the drumstick! "Bandit!" yells Viv as Meg runs off.

Set a Purpose for Reading by Previewing Comprehension Questions

Educators often preview a text with pupils by reviewing the title, looking at the illustrations and activating pupils' background knowledge about the topic. Another tool that supports setting a purpose for reading is reviewing comprehension questions for the group. By referencing the questions throughout the reading process, pupils are encouraged to monitor their comprehension and engage in active reading strategies.

Use Choral or Partner Reading Instead of Round Robin

Instructional approaches that support pupil engagement during story reading are reviewed in Chapter 1 (pages 29 and 32). The three primary engagement techniques are choral reading, partner reading or reading to oneself. These techniques are often interchangeable. Some educators might have all pupils chorally read the first two pages of text and then pair off to partner read the remainder of the story. It is highly recommended that pupils are provided with a chance to individually "preview" the text prior to choral reading using a whisper or quiet voice. That way, they can practise or inquire about challenging words.

Step 10: Applying Phonics Knowledge to Dictation

Pupils benefit from a comprehensive approach that simultaneously supports the development of phonics skills for both word reading and spelling. Therefore, a selection of sounds, words and sentences used for reading have been featured in the dictation portion of the Game Plan. Pupils are practising two new spelling strategies in the current Game Plan. They are learning the rules for using suffix -es and spelling multisyllabic words for the first time.

Dictation Routine for Game Plan

Dictation	Selected Elements
Heart Word	island
Letters/Sounds/ Rime Patterns	-ish, -atch, -oth
Words	dishcloth, picnic, drumstick
Sentence	Meg snatches the drumstick.

WINNING STRATEGY: Spelling Rules for Multisyllabic Short Vowel Words

Pupils often resort to guessing when spelling longer words due to limitations in phonemic awareness, phonics or the lack of a strategic approach. As words increase in length, they typically include more complex syllable patterns, affixes and irregular letter sequences that may be unfamiliar to developing spellers. Research suggests that pupils with weaker phonological awareness may struggle to break down these complex words into manageable parts, causing them to rely on partial phonetic cues or visual approximations rather than accurate spelling rules (Treiman, 1993). As pupils move into spelling two-syllable words, the single most important strategy teachers provide is segmenting the word into individual syllables before attempting to spell sounds. By reinforcing segmentation strategies, teachers help the pupil chunk the word into parts and, similar to reading, increase their accuracy in applying phonics rules. Teachers can guide pupils in spelling multisyllabic words by following this procedure:

1. Model oral syllable division of spelling words using "chin drop".
2. Count the number of syllables. Draw a slash to indicate that there will be two syllables (one on each side of the slash).
3. Pronounce the first syllable.
4. Break up the first syllable into individual sounds. Draw a dash to represent each sound in the syllable, or simply represent each sound with the appropriate letters.
5. Repeat with the second syllable.
6. Guide pupils in checking their spelling of the word one syllable at a time.

Utilise this procedure and the script on page 133 when dictating words with two syllables for the first time. The remaining portion of the dictation routine is unchanged. Refer to Chapter 2 (pages 60–61) for the full teacher script.

Teacher Script for Introducing, Modelling and Practising Spelling Words with Two Syllables

Introduction to Strategy

Teacher: *All words are made up of syllables. Syllables are words or parts of words with one vowel sound. The number of vowel sounds in a word equals the number of syllables. When we spell, first say the word then count the number of syllables in the word.*

Type of Words

Two-Syllable Short Vowel Words Without a Suffix

Teacher: *Your word to spell is "dishcloth".*

Pupils repeat the word.

Teacher: *"Dishcloth" has more than one syllable. Let's count the number of times our chin drops when we say "dishcloth". Two drops means two syllables. "Dishcloth" is a two-syllable word. Let's draw a slash to show there will be two syllables. The first syllable is "dish" with three sounds.*

_ _ _ /

/d/ is spelt with 'd'
/i/ is spelt with 'i'
/sh/ is spelt with 'sh'

Teacher: *The second syllable is "cloth", which is four sounds.* (Write four dashes.)

d i sh / _ _ _ _

/k/ is spelt with 'c'
/l/ is spelt with 'l'
/o/ is spelt with 'o'
/th/ is spelt 'th'

Some pupils may need less scaffolding. For example, they may divide the word into syllables, orally segment the syllables into sounds and then write the corresponding letter to spell the sound.

d i sh / c l o th

Corrective Feedback

If pupils incorrectly write the spelling of a sound or miss a letter, use the following script.

Teacher: *What is the word you are spelling?* (Pupil says word.)

Have the pupil say the sounds and point to the letters that spell each sound. When the pupil points to the incorrect letter(s), use the following script.

Teacher: *You said _______. ________ is spelt ______ in the word _______.* (Pupil corrects misspelling.)

Have the pupil say the sounds and point to the letters again to reinforce the correct spelling.

Proposed Practice Schedule

The practice schedule below suggests one method of arranging the activities into approximately 20-minute lessons over the course of three days. Please note that the first day of the lesson does not include connected text, which is a high-leverage activity for building fluency, and we recommend rereading previously learnt sentences for a quick lesson warm-up.

<table>
<tr><th>Day 1 (18 mins)</th><th>Day 2 (23 mins)</th><th>Day 3 (20 mins)</th></tr>
<tr><td>Phonics Concept
(5 mins)</td><td>Heart Words
(5 mins)</td><td>RAN Chart – Phrases
(5 mins)</td></tr>
<tr><td>Letter/Sound/Rime Review
(3 mins)</td><td>Sentences
(5 mins)</td><td>Dictation
(10 mins)</td></tr>
<tr><td>Single Words
(5 mins)</td><td>Vocabulary
(8 mins)</td><td rowspan="2">Finish Book/
Read Another Book
(5 mins)</td></tr>
<tr><td>RAN Chart – Single Words
(5 mins)</td><td>Book Reading
(5 mins)</td></tr>
</table>

Game Plan

Decodable Text: ***The Muffin Shop,* Dandelion Launchers Units 16–20, Book 17b**
Phonics Concept: **Reading and spelling multisyllabic words with short vowel syllables; syllable division; suffix -s/-es**

Letter/Sound/Rime Review				Phonics Concept
-est	-ess	-og	-ed	Provide direct instruction in the phonics concept, utilising words pulled from the Reader and/or that fit the patterns you are teaching.
-and	-ell	-ish	-in	

Suffix Review

-s	-es

Single Word Reading

finishes	eggshells	muffin	restless

Heart Words

says	go	into	wants

RAN Charts (Single Words & Phrases)

finishes	eggshells	muffin	restless	finishes his muffin	eggshells, salad	hotdogs, sandwiches	is restless
eggshells	finishes	restless	muffin	eggshells, salad	finishes his muffin	is restless	hotdogs, sandwiches
muffin	restless	eggshells	finishes	finishes his muffin	is restless	hotdogs, sandwiches	eggshells, salad
restless	eggshells	muffin	finishes	is restless	hotdogs, sandwiches	eggshells, salad	finishes his muffin

Sentence Reading

Fred finishes his muffin.

He is restless.

Eggshells, salad, hotdogs, sandwiches… Yuck!

Multiple-Meaning Word: tip

Definition 1	Definition 2	Questions
(v) To tilt or push something.	(n) A suggestion or piece of advice.	How might you react if you accidentally tip over a drink? Has anyone ever given you a tip? Did you find the tip helpful?
Sentence 1 The recipe said to tip the milk into the bowl of flour.	**Sentence 2** My art teacher gives me lots of tips about how to paint better.	

Story and Comprehension Questions

What do Fred and Mum have at the muffin shop?	Why does Fred get restless?	What makes Fred realise he put the pad and pen in the bin?

Dictation

Heart Word	wants
Letters/Sounds/Rime Patterns	-and, -ish, -est
Words	finishes, muffin, eggshells
Sentence	Fred is restless.

In practice, RAN phrases should be displayed across a single line.

Chapter 6

Spelling Strategies with Suffixes

- Rules for reading and spelling with suffix -ed
- Syntactic phrasing for sentence reading
- Rules for reading and spelling with suffix -ing

Game Plan

Decodable Text: ***Stranded*, Dandelion Launchers Units 16-20, Book 18a**
Phonics Concept: **Spelling multisyllabic short vowel words with -ed**

Letter/Sound/Rime Review			**Phonics Concept**
br-	gr-	-ump	Provide direct instruction in the phonics concept, utilising words pulled from the Reader and/or that fit the patterns you are teaching.
-en	-an	-unk	

Suffix Review

-ed	-es	-s

Single Word Reading

mittens	jumped	scanned	grabbed

Heart Words

began	onto	along	tree

RAN Charts (Single Words and Phrases)

scanned	mittens	sunlit	jumped	Dennis scanned	licked his mittens	grabbed Dennis	from branch to branch
sunlit	scanned	jumped	mittens	grabbed Dennis	Dennis scanned	from branch to branch	licked his mittens
mittens	jumped	scanned	sunlit	licked his mittens	from branch to branch	Dennis scanned	grabbed Dennis
jumped	sunlit	mittens	scanned	from branch to branch	licked his mittens	grabbed Dennis	Dennis scanned

Sentence Reading

Dennis the kitten licked his mittens.

He scanned the sunlit branches.

Dennis jumped from branch to branch, up and up until he got to the top.

Multiple-Meaning Word: scan

Definition 1 (v) Looking quickly across an area to find a particular object or person.	**Definition 2** (v) Using a machine to look inside like an X-ray.	**Questions** Where might you need to scan a crowd or a place for a person? What is the benefit of being able to scan something you can't see inside of?
Sentence 1 I scan the crowded room, looking for my teacher.	**Sentence 2** At the airport, the X-ray machines scan our bags.	

Story and Comprehension Questions

Why did the branch Dennis was on crack?	Why did the robin have an advantage over Dennis the cat?	In the story, the author writes, "Dennis hatched a plan." What does it mean to hatch a plan?

Dictation

Heart Word	onto
Letters/Sounds/Rime Patterns	-an, -en, -ump
Words	mittens, jumped, grabbed
Sentence	Dennis scanned the sunlit branches.

In practice, RAN phrases should be displayed across a single line.

Target Skills for Game Plan

As texts become more sophisticated, sentence and word complexity increase. For example, sentences that were once simple, brief and often formulaic (e.g. "Tam sat.") are now complex and may vary in phrase structure (e.g. "Dennis jumped from branch to branch, up and up until he got to the top."). Sophisticated sentences that contain multisyllabic words with and without suffixes require different skills for fluency and comprehension. First, ongoing effective instruction in morphology offers guidance on rules for reading and spelling suffixes. In addition, morphology instruction provides the necessary information to determine how suffixes alter the meaning of base words. Furthermore, to comprehend longer sentences and read them with intonation, pupils rely on syntactic knowledge to parse the text into meaningful phrases. Accordingly, there are three target skills for the current Game Plan:

- Syntactic phrasing for sentence reading
- Introducing the purpose and spelling rules for suffix -ed
- Introducing the purpose and spelling rules for suffix -ing

By providing explicit instruction that supports pupils' phrasing of text and spelling rules for the addition of common suffixes such as -ed and -ing, instructors support pupils' accuracy, automaticity and comprehension.

Your Team

Pupils are ready for this lesson when they have demonstrated accuracy and fluency when reading single- and multi-syllable short vowel words, including those with beginning and ending adjacent consonants. Once pupils have mastered these more complex rime patterns and starter sounds, they are ready for words with additional complexities, including words with suffixes beyond suffix -s and -es.

Case Study

You provide targeted Structured Literacy lessons to small groups based on instructional focus areas identified through screening data. One "at risk" pupil, Elijah, is a strong speller. He demonstrates solid grapheme-phoneme correspondences, but when reading aloud, you note that he sounds "staccato". When responding to comprehension questions, it is clear that Elijah has difficulty monitoring for comprehension. Another pupil, Nina, uses appropriate intonation when reading aloud. However, her reading is slow and laboured. You are concerned that her slow pace will impact her comprehension with complex texts. When spelling, Nina demonstrates difficulty with words that are multisyllabic and include suffixes. What strategies can help Elijah and Nina develop their reading skills to move closer to benchmark reading proficiency?

Your Equipment

The Game Plan in Chapter 6 targets several different areas of skill building. The current Game Plan addresses syntactic phrasing, or the ways in which sentences are structured, along with the pronunciation and spelling rules for suffix -ed. This Game Plan is based on the text *Stranded* (Book 18a) from the **Dandelion Launchers Units 16-20** series. Rather than using one Game Plan as a platform for practice, as was the case with previous chapters, educators will use different Game Plans provided in this chapter to support the application of different skills.

Series: Dandelion Launchers Units 16-20
(ISBN 9781783693337)
Reader: *Stranded*
(Book 18a)
Phonics Concept:
Spelling multisyllabic short vowel words; -ed with doubling.
Book Overview:
A confident cat over-estimates his hunting skills and finds himself in a tricky situation.

Text from the Book *Stranded*

Dennis the kitten licked his mittens. He scanned the sunlit branches.

Dennis spotted a robin. "I am a big cat. I can hunt," he bragged to himself.

Dennis hatched a plan. He jumped onto the tree trunk and ran along the branch.

Dennis jumped from branch to branch, up and up until he got to the top.

He inched along the thin branch. It cracked! Dennis began to swing! PANIC! HELP!

All of a sudden, a hand grabbed Dennis. "Ha! Ha! Can't get me!" chanted the robin.

Additional Texts

The additional Game Plan for Chapter 6 addresses syntactic phrasing and the spelling rules for suffix -ing (there is only one pronunciation) and is based on the text *Thinking of a Gift* (Book 19a) from Dandelion **Launchers Units 16-20**.

Depending on the skill level of your pupils, it may be necessary to provide additional opportunities for practice beyond the Game Plans in this chapter. For recommendations on texts to form the basis for crafting your own additional Game Plans, see **Additional Texts for Applying Reading and Spelling Skills for Suffix -ed** and **Additional Texts for Applying Reading and Spelling Skills for Suffix -ing** on page 140.

Additional Texts for Applying Reading and Spelling Skills for Suffix -ed

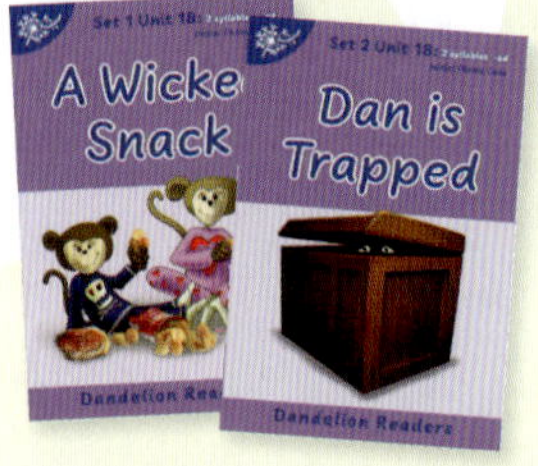

The **Dandelion Readers Set 1 Units 11-20** (Book 18) (ISBN 9781907170058), **Dandelion Readers Set 2 Units 11-20** (Book 18) (ISBN 9781907170065) and **Dandelion World Stages 16-20** (Books 18a and 18b) (ISBN 9780241666715) series target the same phonics concept as the **Dandelion Launchers Units 16-20** (Books 18a and 18b) series, thereby providing the opportunity for instruction and application in additional texts before moving on to the next phonics concept.

Additional Texts for Applying Reading and Spelling Skills for Suffix -ing

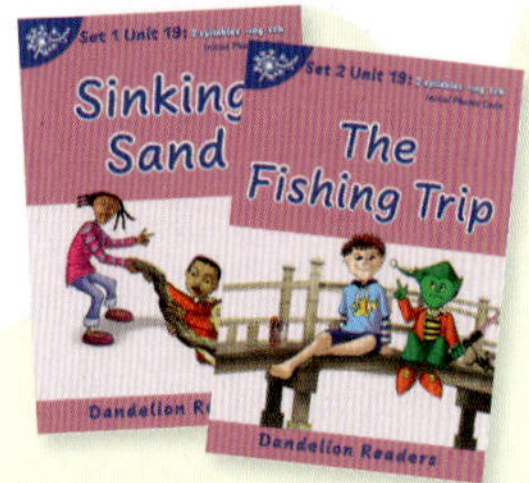

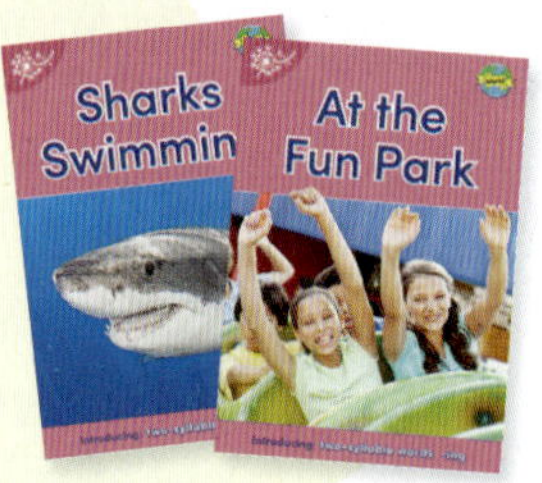

The **Dandelion Readers Set 1 Units 11-20** (Book 19) (ISBN 9781907170058), **Dandelion Readers Set 2 Units 11-20** (Book 19) (ISBN 9781907170065) and **Dandelion World Stages 16-20** (Books 19a and 19b) (ISBN 9780241666715) series target the same phonics concept as the **Dandelion Launchers Units 16-20** (Books 19a and 19b) series, thereby providing the opportunity for instruction and application in additional texts before moving on to the next phonics concept.

Planning for Game Day

The Game Plan in Chapter 6 was designed using the same backwards planning approach as Chapters 1–5. Backwards planning ensures the activities in the Structured Literacy routines are aligned with patterns, vocabulary and text pupils will encounter in the accompanying book. The sequence for backwards planning is shared in the following breakout box on page 141.

Backwards Planning Using a Decodable Text

Planning Reading Activities (Sentences, Single Words, RAN Charts and Suffixes)

Step 1: Choose three sentences from the text. Select sentences that offer practice for target phonics skills.

Step 2: Select four individual words for single word reading. These words should offer practice with the target phonics skills and preferably appear in the sentences.

Step 3: Use the individual words and phrases from the sentences to create RAN charts.

Step 4: Choose suffixes to teach sound-symbol correspondence.

Planning Heart Word and Dictation Activity

Step 1: Choose up to four irregular/heart words to practise, preferably from the text.

Step 2: Plan your dictation task by selecting rime patterns, one heart word, three single words and at least one sentence from the previous reading activities for dictation tasks.

Planning Vocabulary and Comprehension Activities

Step 1: Choose one multiple-meaning vocabulary word from the book for instruction.

Step 2: Read the text and craft questions that require pupils to find the information in the text (factual questions), analyse word meaning (semantic questions) or "read between the lines" to understand the deeper purpose of the story (inference questions). Set a purpose for reading by providing a question for pupils to keep in mind as they read the book.

Winning Strategies

The instructional routines in the Game Plan support developing pupils' ability to accurately read and spell words with suffixes -ed and -ing. Furthermore, the syntactic phrasing strategy supports the development of automatic phrasing and expression when reading sentences and longer passages.

- Rules for reading and spelling with suffix -ed
- Syntactic phrasing for sentence reading
- Rules for reading and spelling with suffix -ing

Rules for Reading and Spelling with Suffix -ed

Teaching the suffix -ed in an explicit and systematic manner supports understanding the purpose of the suffix, the appropriate pronunciation and the rules related to spelling. The most straightforward aspect of suffix -ed is the way it changes the meaning of a base word. Suffix -ed is added to a verb to mean occurring in the past. The suffix is unique because it can be pronounced in three different ways, /ed/, /d/ or /t/, depending on the sounds in the base word. Furthermore, suffix -ed can impact the spelling of base words because, in some cases, it may require the addition of a second consonant letter to preserve the pronunciation of the vowel. For example, to preserve the short vowel sound /o/ in the word "hop", the consonant is doubled before -ed is added, creating the past tense of the word "hop" (hopped). If the consonant was not properly doubled, in this example the resulting word would be "hoped".

Syntactic Phrasing for Sentence Reading

Syntactic knowledge, or the understanding of sentence structure and parts of speech, is a foundational component of reading fluency and comprehension (Nation & Snowling, 2000). When children understand that words have jobs and that different words work together to create phrases, they are able to read with greater fluency and increased comprehension. For example, most English sentences follow a sequence in which verbs occur after subjects. Knowledge of typical syntactic structures helps pupils anticipate the flow of information, which enhances their reading fluency. In other words, understanding syntax helps pupils predict the relationships between words and their roles within a sentence. This offers a "roadmap" to the reader, which increases fluency. Furthermore, syntactic knowledge enhances comprehension by helping pupils navigate complex sentences.

Teaching parts of speech and sentence structure also equips pupils to decode unfamiliar words based on context. For example, in the sentence "The famished children quickly ate their entire lunch", the adjective "famished" may be unfamiliar, but the predicate phrase helps decipher the term as similar to "hungry". As a predictive skill, syntactic knowledge reduces cognitive load, enabling readers to focus on meaning rather than struggling to parse each sentence. In fact, one study that examined the relationship between syntactic knowledge and reading fluency in pupils (aged 11 and a half years old on average) found that children's knowledge of parts of speech enhances reading automaticity and comprehension, even when controlling for decoding ability (Mokhtari & Thompson, 2006). In the current chapter, teachers instruct pupils in breaking up sentences into syntactic phrases to enhance pupils' fluency and comprehension skills at the sentence level prior to reading the whole book.

Rules for Spelling with Suffix -ing

Although it is not as complex as suffix -ed, instruction on the spelling rules for suffix -ing provides important reading and writing support for pupils. When added to a base word, suffix -ing forms the present participle, or gerund, form of the verb, indicating ongoing or continuous action. The challenge with suffix -ing most often occurs during spelling. At this point, pupils must determine whether or not to adjust the spelling of the base word when adding the suffix. As a general rule, spelling changes occur in order to preserve the syllable type and associated vowel pronunciation of the base word. For example, when suffix -ing is added to words with two letters in the rime pattern, the reader requires a pronunciation cue to appropriately pronounce the vowel's short sound (tap + ing = tapping). That cue is the double final letter. Otherwise, readers might confuse the pronunciation of short vowel words with two-letter rime patterns and split vowel spelling words, particularly because when split vowel spelling words words add suffixes, the final 'e' is dropped (tape + ing = taping). The same confusion does not occur with short vowel words with three letters in the rime pattern (e.g. stick, band, bless) because there are very few split vowel spelling words that have adjacent consonants or a digraph in the rime pattern (e.g. cache, paste). By doubling the final letter of appropriate short rime patterns, pupils can ensure the correct pronunciation of the vowel sound.

Rime Patterns Streamline Spelling with Suffixes

By capitalising on pupils' knowledge of rime patterns, instruction in spelling rules that govern the addition of suffixes can be streamlined. For example, when determining whether the consonant needs to be doubled when adding vowel suffixes such as -ing, directing pupils' attention to the rime pattern can be helpful. Pupils should ask themselves:

1. Does the rime pattern have a short vowel?
2. Does the rime pattern have only two letters?

If the answer to both of those questions is yes, then the final consonant should be doubled when adding a vowel suffix.

Step 1: Teach Phonics Concepts Using Winning Strategies

The phonics concepts for this chapter include reading and spelling multisyllabic words with suffix -ed and -ing. Instructions for reading multisyllabic words with -ed are presented in this section of the chapter because of the complexities involved with the task.

WINNING STRATEGY: Rules for Reading Words with Suffix -ed

Suffix -ed can be pronounced as three different sounds: /ed/, /d/ or /t/. The pronunciation of the suffix is complex because of the process of coarticulation, or the manner in which one speech sound is influenced by the letters that precede it. All suffixes are coarticulated with the ending of a base word.

First Sound: /ed/

When suffix -ed follows a base word that ends with either 'd' (e.g. land/landed, pad/padded) or 't' (e.g. plant/planted, support/supported), the suffix is pronounced /ed/. This pronunciation can sometimes sound like /id/ when articulated. The pronunciation switch is related to the final 'd' and 't' in the word. These letters are paired voiced and unvoiced sounds. Paired sounds imply the two sounds share a manner and place of articulation. In the case of 'd' and 't', the tongue is pressed against the bumpy part of the roof of the mouth behind the teeth, called the alveolar ridge. By creating a seal between the tongue and the roof of the mouth, the sound is produced by releasing a burst of breath. When the base word ends with 'd' or 't', the final tongue positioning makes it difficult to enunciate another similar sound (e.g. /ed/). This is the reason the vowel sound in suffix -ed can sometimes resemble /i/ rather than /e/.

Second Sound: /d/

When the base word ends with a final voiced sound other than 'd' or 't', the /d/ sound is clearly articulated, and the additional vowel sound /e/ is not necessary. Therefore, suffix -ed makes a /d/ sound when it is coarticulated with base words that end with a voiced sound (e.g. rave/raved; club/clubbed; praise/praised).

Third Sound: /t/

When the suffix -ed is coarticulated with a base word that ends in an unvoiced sound (e.g. swish/swished; lick/licked), it is pronounced with a /t/ sound. The /t/ sound occurs in these circumstances because shifting from the pronunciation of an unvoiced sound to a /d/ sound is rather challenging. Try it with the word "bump". Force yourself to make the /d/ sound at the end of the base word – /bumpd/. You should find this difficult. In order to articulate efficiently, a shortcut results in the pronunciation of suffix -ed as /t/, which improves the overall fluency of reading and speaking these words.

Teacher Script for Introducing and Practising the Pronunciation of the Three Sounds of Suffix -ed

Introduction to Strategy

Teacher: *Today, we will continue our discussion of suffixes. These word parts can be attached to base words and have the power to change their meaning and pronunciation.*

Type of Words

Single-Syllable Short Vowel Words with Rebellious Rime Patterns (CVCC Words)

Introduce Purpose and Pronunciation of Suffix -ed

Write "-ed" on the board.

Teacher: *Here is the suffix -ed. When suffix -ed is added to a word, it places the word in the past tense. The tricky thing is that -ed can be pronounced in three different ways. The pronunciation relies on the sounds at the end of the base word.*

Additional Words to Practise Reading

Draw a three-column table with headings that represent the three sounds of suffix -ed.

/ed/	/d/	/t/

First Sound of Suffix -ed: /ed/

Teacher: *When the base word ends with a 'd' or 't', the suffix is pronounced /ed/. For example, let's add suffix -ed to the base word "frost": frost + ed = frosted.*

Second Sound of Suffix -ed: /d/

Teacher: *When the base word ends with a voiced final sound, the suffix makes the /d/ sound. For example, let's add suffix -ed to the base word "fill": fill + ed = filled.*

Third Sound of Suffix -ed: /t/

Teacher: *When the base word ends with an unvoiced final sound, then the suffix makes the /t/ sound. For example, let's add the suffix -ed to the base word "pick": pick + ed = picked.*

Additional Words to Sort by Suffix -ed Sound

Have pupils sort additional words into the correct pronunciation column on the table you have already started.

/ed/	/d/	/t/
hunted folded	bugged jazzed	plumped brushed

The instructions for reading multisyllabic words with suffix -ing are presented in Step 3 (**Reinforce Suffix Pronunciations in Isolation**). When teaching pupils the three sounds of suffix -ed, it may be helpful to break up the instruction over several days. It also may be helpful to review the difference between voiced and unvoiced sounds.

Step 2: Reinforce Letters/Sounds in Isolation

The Game Plans include activities for practising consonants, vowels, digraphs, adjacent consonants, rime patterns and affixes in isolation. Teaching familiar letter patterns such as rime units, adjacent consonants and affixes facilitates the recognition of word parts and enables greater automaticity in word recognition and spelling. The Game Plan features the isolated practice of two Sticky Starters and four rime patterns featured in the book *Stranded.*

Letter/Sound/Rime Review for Game Plan

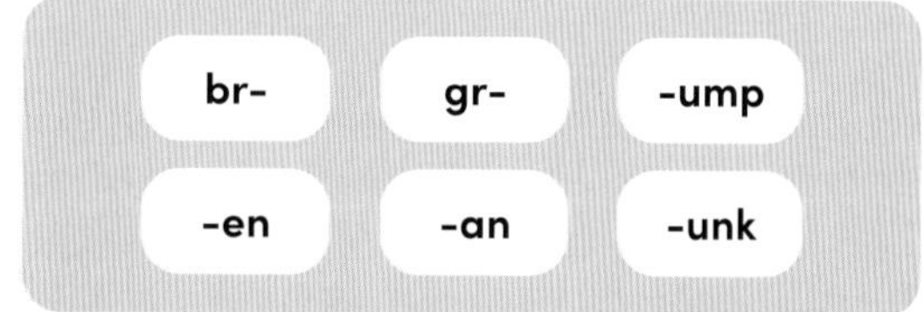

Step 3: Reinforce Suffix Pronunciations in Isolation

The current Game Plan incorporates an isolated review of previously taught suffixes. During the review, instruction elicits knowledge of suffix spelling, purpose and varied pronunciations. In the current lesson, pupils will review the new suffix, -ed, as well as previously taught suffixes, -s and -es.

The suffix -ing is an important component of the additional Game Plan designed to accompany the text *Thinking of a Gift.* The suffix is introduced and practised following the same protocols used in Chapter 4 (pages 97–99).

Suffix Review for Game Plan

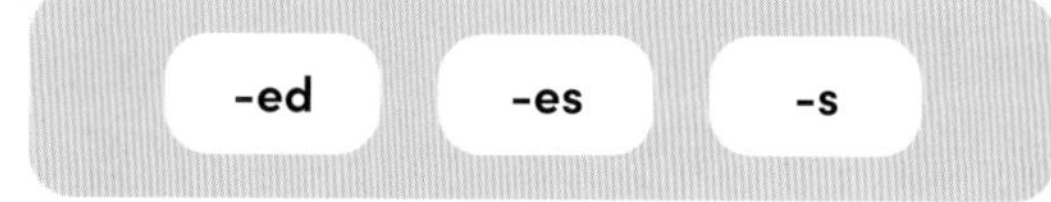

Introducing Suffix -ing

Introduction to Strategy

Teacher: *We have a new suffix to learn. It is "-ing".*

Type of Suffixes

Single-Syllable Short Vowel Words with Suffix -ing

Introduce Purpose and Pronunciation of Suffix -ing

Write "-ing" on the board.

Teacher: *Here is the suffix -ing. It is spelt I-N-G and is pronounced "-ing".*

Elicit correct pronunciation.

Teacher: *When suffix -ing is added to verbs, it ensures they are in the present tense.*

Additional Practice

1. swim + ing = swimming
2. run + ing = running
3. hunt + ing = hunting
4. jump + ing = jumping
5. sob + ing = sobbing

Step 4: Apply Phonics Concept to Single Words from the Text

The Game Plan features four words from the text *Stranded*. Each word includes the target reading skill – decoding multisyllabic words with a suffix.

Individual Words for Game Plan

mittens | jumped | scanned | grabbed

Practise Reading Words with Suffixes

After teaching the spelling, pronunciation and purpose of suffixes, include activities that ensure accurate and automatic word reading. Some pupils apply their knowledge of suffixes seamlessly. Others require a structured or scaffolded approach. (See the **Teacher Script for Reading Words by Base, Affix and in Combined Form** on page 148 for a demonstration.) Although this step may be unnecessary, it becomes a helpful tool as the spelling of the base word is impacted by the presence of the suffix – for example, in words where the final letter is dropped (e.g. tape/taping) or changed (e.g. dry/dried). In these cases, a visual that depicts the base word in its original form (tape) and the compounded form (taping) reminds pupils that even when spellings shift, pronunciation remains the same.

Teacher Script for Reading Words by Base, Affix and in Combined Form

Introduction to Strategy

Teacher: *Let's practise reading words with our new prefix/suffix. I will read the base word, pronounce the prefix/suffix, then combine them into the final word.*

Teacher Models	Base Word	Prefix or Suffix	Complete Word
Teacher Models	mitten	-s	mittens
Teacher and Pupils Together	jump	-s	jumps
Pupils Alone	scan	-ed	scanned
Pupils Alone	grab	-ed	grabbed

Providing Additional Support for Reading Multisyllabic Words with Suffixes

Some pupils may be able to automatically decode multisyllabic words, while others will require ongoing support. Here's a quick reminder of the steps involved.

1. Circle any suffixes and save for later reading.
2. Find and dot the letters making vowel sounds in the base word.
3. Underline the rime pattern.
4. Divide between rime patterns.
5. Backwards decode the word, reading the final syllable first.
6. Blend the syllables and pronounce the whole base word.
7. Pronounce the suffix.
8. Combine the base word and suffix.

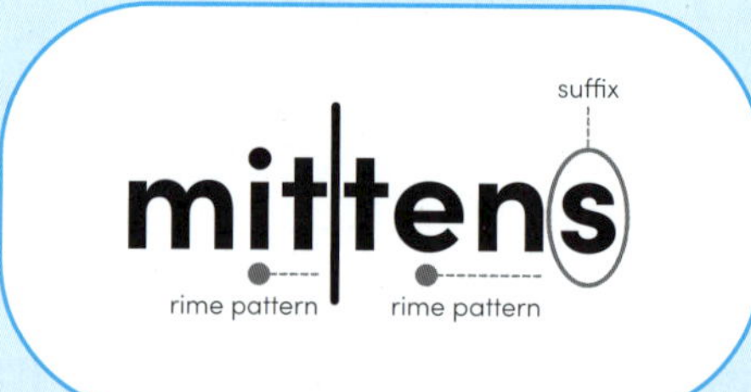

Step 5: Build Knowledge of Heart Words

The Game Plan has selected four heart words from the text *Stranded*. As texts become longer and more complex, heart words may increase in length. Three of the chosen heart words are two syllables (e.g. began, onto, along). The instructional strategy for teaching a two-syllable word relies on the oral segmentation of syllables using the chin drop method. See Chapter 5 (page 128) for additional information on two-syllable heart word instruction. The final heart word, "tree", is included because while pupils may have had instruction in the digraph 'ee', they may need additional practice to spell accurately. Educators can use their discretion about whether or not to teach "tree" as a heart word.

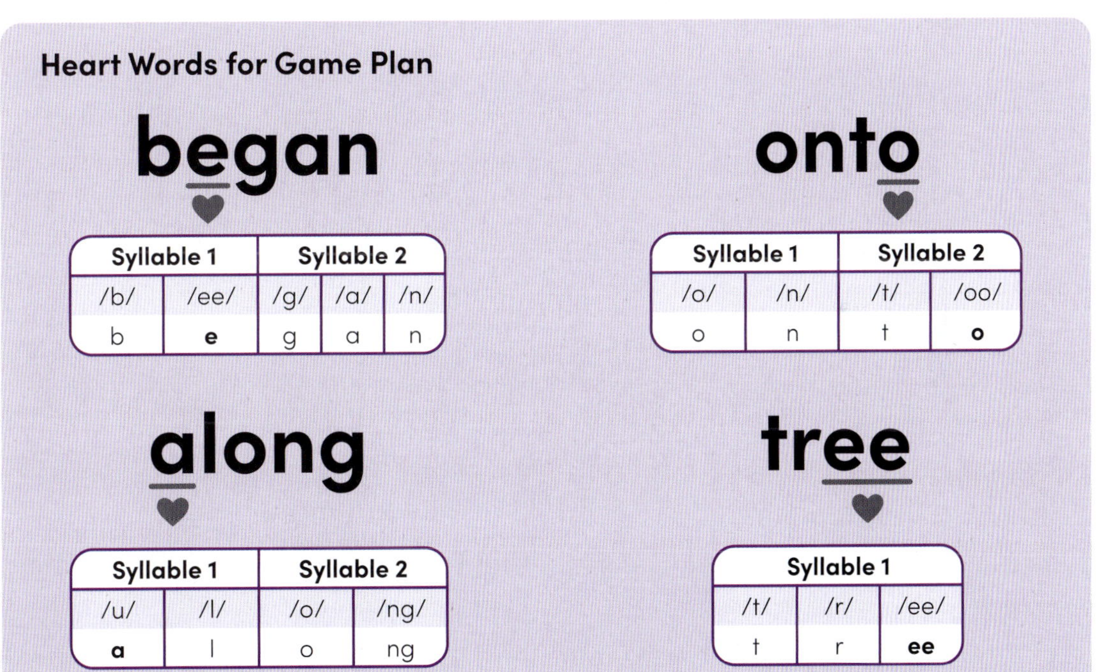

Step 6: Enhance Sight Word Recognition with RAN Charts

The Game Plan RAN charts include the individual words and phrases featured in other parts of the lesson. RAN charts are a Winning Strategy from Chapter 3 and are used to practise the automatic retrieval of common single words and phrases. They support tracking across a page and the "return sweep" to the next line.

RAN Charts for Game Plan

Dennis scanned	licked his mittens	grabbed Dennis	from branch to branch
grabbed Dennis	Dennis scanned	from branch to branch	licked his mittens
licked his mittens	from branch to branch	Dennis scanned	grabbed Dennis
from branch to branch	licked his mittens	grabbed Dennis	Dennis scanned

scanned	mittens	sunlit	jumped
sunlit	scanned	jumped	mittens
mittens	jumped	scanned	sunlit
jumped	sunlit	mittens	scanned

Step 7: Practise Reading Sentences from the Text

The current Game Plan has selected the following sentences from the text *Stranded* because they include multisyllabic words and words with suffixes.

Sentences for Game Plan

Dennis the kitten licked his mittens.
He scanned the sunlit branches.
Dennis jumped from branch to branch, up and up until he got to the top.

WINNING STRATEGY: Syntactic Phrasing for Sentence Reading

A Structured Literacy framework is valuable for lesson planning because it includes instruction on multiple aspects of word knowledge. Previous chapters have focused on building abilities in phonemic awareness, phonics, semantics and morphology. In Chapter 4 (page 96), there is a brief discussion about parts of speech to support understanding of the morphology. However, this chapter integrates robust teaching on syntax. Syntactic knowledge offers a roadmap that allows pupils to predict word order, support automaticity and improve overall fluency and comprehension.

Step-by-Step Instruction for Teaching Syntactic Phrasing

Syntactic phrasing describes an approach to reading that emphasises the structure and purpose of the sentence. In order to support pupils' knowledge of syntax, instruction simultaneously describes parts of speech and common phrase structures, and also supports application to sentences from the book. During the activity, teachers will visually illustrate the syntactic structure of the sentence by "scooping" words into their phrases (segmenting the phrases of the sentence with underlines). Common phrasing structures include the subject phrase, predicate/verb phrase, prepositional phrase, conjunctions and additional clauses or objects. Pupils are guided to follow the scoops as they read sentences aloud. It is helpful for pupils to have a personal copy of the sentences for scooping and reading. This pedagogical scaffold supports the development of prosody, or intonation, and comprehension during reading.

Furthermore, in order to support pupils' comprehension and knowledge of syntax, teachers ask a series of comprehension questions that inquire about the different elements of the sentence. For example, "Who or what is the sentence about? What is the subject doing? When, where or how is the action taking place?"

Common Phrases to Support Syntactic Knowledge

Subject Phrase

A subject phrase describes who/what the sentence is about. It may include more than one subject or describer word (e.g. adjectives).

Predicate or Verb Phrase

A predicate describes the action of the subject(s). A verb phrase may include description words (e.g. adverbs) or modifiers (e.g. can, has).

Conjunction

A conjunction is a word or phrase that connects two ideas (e.g. and, but, so, unless).

Prepositional Phrase

A prepositional phrase is a phrase that begins with a preposition and describes or modifies the subject, predicate noun or verb.

Additional Clause or Object

In compound sentences, a subordinate clause further describes the predicate. An object is the person/thing that receives the effect of the predicate or subordinate clause.

Examples of phrasing structures in sample sentences:

The small pink pig **Subject**	rolled **Predicate**	in the mud. **Preposition**

Two chipmunks, Fred and Rocket, **Preposition**	hunted for nuts **Subject**	until **Predicate**	the sun set. **Conjunction**

On top of the cliff, **Preposition**	the chicks **Subject**	sat **Predicate**	in the nest. **Preposition**

Teacher Script for Syntactic Phrasing During Sentence Reading

Introduction to Strategy

Teacher: *We are going to read some sentences. First, we will read the sentence quietly, then I will show you how to break it into phrases. Next, we will practise reading the phrases. Finally, I will ask you comprehension questions about the sentence.*

Introduce Purpose and Approach to Syntactic Phrasing

Write or project the sentence "Dennis the kitten licked his mittens."

Teacher: *First, I would like you to read the sentence quietly.*

Elicit silent reading from pupils.

Teacher: *Now, watch me break up the sentence into phrases.*

Scoop underneath the phrases shown below to break up the sentence. Describe the type of phrase as necessary.

Dennis the kitten	licked	his mittens.
Subject	**Predicate**	**Object**

Teacher: *Please copy the phrase scoops onto your sheet. It's your turn to read as a group.*

Pupils chorally read aloud, following the teacher's pointer/finger as each phrase is scooped.

Teacher: *I have a few questions to ask you about this sentence.*

Use the following prompts as appropriate:

Who is this sentence about? (Subject phrase.)

What happened to ___? (Predicate phrase.)

Where, when or how did it happen? (Prepositional phrase.)

Did anything else happen to the subject? (For compound sentences.)

What are you picturing in your mind? (Visualisation strategy.)

Repeat steps as appropriate for remaining sentences.

Additional Practice

A suggested syntactic structure for additional sentences is offered below. Sentences may be simplified or modified for this activity.

Dennis	scanned	the sunlit branches.
Subject	**Predicate**	**Object**

All of a sudden,	a hand	grabbed	Dennis.
Preposition	**Subject**	**Predicate**	**Object**

Tips for Differentiating Syntactic Phrasing

If the skills of your pupils vary significantly, then you may want to use some of the differentiation strategies listed below.

Modelling Fluency

Teachers begin instruction in syntactic phrasing by asking pupils to read the sentence quietly. Then, teachers model how to scoop the phrases in the sentence (teachers should avoid reading the sentence aloud during this step). Finally, teachers run their finger/pointer along each scoop as pupils chorally read the phrases aloud.

Encourage Visualisation

Teachers can support the development of advanced comprehension skills by asking pupils what they visualise as they read each sentence, pointing pupils back to the text to find evidence.

Allowing Pupils to Create Their Own Phrases

Teachers can provide a blank copy of sentences from the text, which offers the perfect platform for advanced pupils to work together in pairs or individually to demonstrate their own knowledge of phrasing. It can be helpful to ask the pupils to familiarise themselves with the sentence by reading it before scooping it.

Connect to Wave 1 Instruction

It might be helpful to utilise writing curriculum resources that introduce the different parts of speech in this section of the lesson plan.

Step 8: Expand Text-Related Vocabulary Knowledge

Activating pupils' knowledge of multiple-meaning words from the text supports the development of their word recognition skills. The word "scan" is the multiple-meaning word used in the current Game Plan to deepen pupils' vocabulary knowledge and enhance their associations.

Vocabulary Word for Game Plan

Vocabulary Term

scan

Pupil-Friendly Definition 1

Looking quickly across an area to find a particular object or person. (verb)

Using the Term in a Sentence

I scan the crowded room, looking for my teacher.

Pupil-Friendly Definition 2

Using a machine to look inside something. (verb)

Using the Term in a Sentence

At the airport, the X-ray machines scan our bags.

Questions for Discussion

- Where might you need to scan a crowd for a person?
- What is the benefit of being able to scan something you can't see inside of?

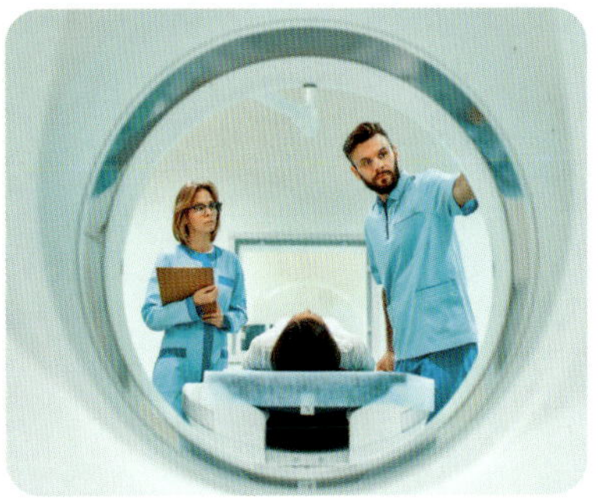

Step 9: Putting It All Together for Text Reading and Comprehension

This activity supports both book reading and comprehension. Although the book is controlled to act as a platform for building word recognition skills with multisyllabic words with suffixes, the text also offers opportunities to engage in meaningful discussion about comprehension. The following questions have been generated for the Game Plan and the text *Stranded*. Additional strategies that enhance comprehension monitoring include activating background knowledge by previewing the title and book illustrations and setting a purpose for reading. See Chapter 1 (pages 29 and 32) for further guidance.

Comprehension Questions for Game Plan

Inferential
Why did the branch Dennis was on crack?

Inferential
Why did the robin have an advantage over Dennis the cat?

Vocabulary in Context
In the story, the author writes, "Dennis hatched a plan." What does it mean to hatch a plan?

Text from the Book *Stranded*
Dennis the kitten licked his mittens. He scanned the sunlit branches.
Dennis spotted a robin. "I am a big cat. I can hunt," he bragged to himself.
Dennis hatched a plan. He jumped onto the tree trunk and ran along the branch.
Dennis jumped from branch to branch, up and up until he got to the top.
He inched along the thin branch. It cracked! Dennis began to swing! PANIC! HELP!
All of a sudden, a hand grabbed Dennis. "Ha! Ha! Can't get me!" chanted the robin.

Step 10: Applying Phonics Knowledge to Dictation

WINNING STRATEGY: Spelling with Suffix -ed

Spelling words with suffixes is often complicated because writing the whole word is not simply a matter of adding the suffix. Rather, the addition of most suffixes requires a modification to the spelling of the base word. As a general rule, spelling changes occur to the base word in order to preserve the original syllable type and pronunciation of the vowel.

Pupils benefit from a comprehensive approach that simultaneously supports the development of phonics skills for both word reading and spelling. Therefore, a selection of sounds, words and sentences used for reading have been featured in the dictation portion of the Game Plan. The dictation activity provides an opportunity to reinforce spelling single and multisyllabic words, as well as the strategy for spelling with suffix -ed.

Dictation Routine for Game Plan

Dictation	Selected Elements
Heart Word	onto
Letters/Sounds/ Rime Patterns	-an, -en, -ump
Words	mittens, jumped, grabbed
Sentence	Dennis scanned the sunlit branches.

Step-by-Step Instruction for Spelling with Suffix -ed

The first and most common spelling rule for adding suffix -ed is determining whether to double the final letter of the base word. One effective way for teaching this rule is to prompt pupils with a series of questions.

1. Does the base word have a short vowel?
2. Does the rime pattern have only two letters?

If the answer to both questions is yes, then double the final letter before adding the suffix. Practising with spelling suffix -ed words is a productive activity that either occurs the day before the traditional dictation exercise or precedes the dictation activity.

Teacher Script to Practise Spelling with Suffix -ed

Instruction	Teacher Models	Teacher and Pupils Together	Pupils Alone	Pupils Alone	Pupils Alone
Present base word	Let's add -ed to the word "nap".	Let's add -ed to the word "duck".	Let's add -ed to the word "stop".	Let's add -ed to the word "fill".	Let's add -ed to the word "clap".
Model "think aloud" for doubling rule	Does the base word have a short vowel? (yes) Does the rime pattern have two letters? (yes)	Does the base word have a short vowel? (yes) Does the rime pattern have two letters? (no)	Does the base word have a short vowel? (yes) Does the rime pattern have two letters? (yes)	Does the base word have a short vowel? (yes) Does the rime pattern have two letters? (no)	Does the base word have a short vowel? (yes) Does the rime pattern have two letters? (yes)
What's the doubling decision?	Yes, double the last letter – "napped".	No, do not double the last letter – "ducked".	Yes, double the last letter – "stopped".	No, do not double the last letter – "filled".	Yes, double the last letter – "clapped".

When delivering the dictation activity, educators may find the following script useful. See Chapter 5 (page 128) to review the suggested teacher language for prompting children to spell multisyllabic heart words and short vowel words.

Teacher Script for Prompted Strategy During Dictation

Teacher Prompt for Spelling Words with Suffixes

Teacher: *Your word to spell is ________.* (jumped)

Pupils repeat the word.

Teacher: *This is a word with the suffix -ed. Let's spell and write our base word first. Whenever we spell a word with the suffix -ed, we have to ask two questions.*

1. Does the base word have a short vowel?
2. Does the rime pattern have only two letters?

Teacher: *If the answer to both questions is yes, we double the last letter. The word "jump" has three letters in the rime pattern, so we do not double the final letter. We can just add the -ed.*

Repeat with the word "grabbed".

Proposed Practice Schedule

The Game Plan designed to support pupils at this phase of word reading development is broken into 10 steps. The plan has been broken up over the course of four days to keep sessions under 30 minutes. As always, when modifying the schedule, it is recommended that opportunities to apply skills to connected text are prioritised. It should be noted that on Days 1 and 4, connected text practice has not been identified. Teachers will want to identify appropriate texts to include on these days.

Day 1 (25 mins)		Day 2 (18 mins)		Day 3 (20 mins)	Day 4 (10 mins)
Phonics Concept (15 mins)	Suffix Review (3 mins)	RAN Chart – Single Words (3 mins)	Vocabulary (5 mins)	RAN Chart – Phrases (5 mins)	Dictation (10 mins)
				Book Reading and Comprehension (5 mins)	
Letter/Sound/ Rime Review (2 mins)	Single Words (5 mins)	Heart Words (5 mins)	Sentences (5 mins)	Practising Spelling with Suffixes (10 mins)	

Game Plan

Decodable Text: ***Thinking of a Gift*, Dandelion Launchers Units 16-20, Book 19a**
Phonics Concept: **Spelling multisyllabic short vowel words with -ing**

Letter/Sound/Rime Review			Phonics Concept
-ink	-itch	-isk	Provide direct instruction in the phonics concept, utilising words pulled from the Reader and/or that fit the patterns you are teaching.
-an	-ush	-ank	

Suffix Review

-ing	-ed	-s

Single Word Reading

stitching	getting	fixing	thinking

Heart Words

says	into	coming	are

RAN Charts (Single Words and Phrases)

stitching	fixing	thinking	getting	stitching this fabric	fixing flapjacks	thinking of a present	getting Hank
fixing	stitching	getting	thinking	thinking of a present	stitching this fabric	getting Hank	fixing flapjacks
thinking	getting	stitching	fixing	fixing flapjacks	getting Hank	stitching this fabric	thinking of a present
getting	fixing	thinking	stitching	getting Hank	thinking of a present	fixing flapjacks	stitching this fabric

Sentence Reading

"I am getting Hank a pan and a rolling pin," Alf says.

"I am stitching this fabric into a hat," says Stan.

"I am fixing flapjacks for my pals," says Hank.

Multiple-Meaning Word: present

Definition 1 (n) Happening now.	**Definition 2** (n) A gift.	**Questions** What types of objects do we have in the present that we did not have 100 years ago? When might you receive presents?
Sentence 1 In the past, I went to bed at 7pm, but in the present I sleep at 8pm.	**Sentence 2** Amelia made a present for her mother's birthday.	

Story and Comprehension Questions

Why might Hank's pals be getting him gifts?	What do we know about Hank?	What is a synonym for "present"? What are some other meanings of the word?

Dictation

Heart Word	coming
Letters/Sounds/Rime Patterns	-ink, -itch, -ank
Words	thinking, getting, stitching
Sentence	"I am fixing flapjacks for my pals," says Hank.

In practice, RAN phrases should be displayed across a single line.

Chapter 7

Decoding New Vowel Sounds

- Backwards decoding split vowel spelling words
- Decoding multisyllabic words with short and long vowel sounds
- Spelling split vowel spelling words with suffixes using the drop 'e' rule

Game Plan

Decodable Text: ***Late*, Dandelion Readers Split Vowel Spellings, Book 1**
Phonics Concept: **Rime pattern recognition of split vowel spelling words; closed/split vowel spelling syllable division; drop 'e'**

Letter/Sound/Rime Review			Phonics Concept
-ake	-ate	-ave	Provide direct instruction in the phonics concept, utilising words pulled from the Reader and/or that fit the patterns you are teaching.
-ank	-ell	-ame	

Suffix Review

-ed	-s	-ing

Single Word Reading

game	mates	cake	saved

Heart Words

school	said	they	was

RAN Charts (Single Words and Phrases)

game	mates	cake	saved	lost the game	saved the day	his mates	no cake left
cake	game	saved	mates	his mates	lost the game	no cake left	lost the game
mates	saved	game	cake	saved the day	no cake left	lost the game	his mates
saved	cake	saved	game	no cake left	lost the game	his mates	saved the day

Sentence Reading

His team lost the game.

Frank was not late for the game!

Frank's mates yelled, "Frank saved the day!"

Multiple-Meaning Word: game

Definition 1	Definition 2	Questions
(n) An activity or sport where you follow rules and try to win.	(adj) You are willing to try something new.	What kinds of games do people play? When playing a game, what are some things you might need? Where do people play games? What are some things that you might be game to do?
Sentence 1 Her football game was postponed due to bad weather.	**Sentence 2** He said he was game for a road trip to a new place.	

Story and Comprehension Questions

What seems to be a problematic pattern for Frank?	Why did Frank receive an alarm clock from Beth?	At the end of the story, Frank's pals say he "saved the day". About what other character in the story could this term be used?

Dictation

Heart Word	school
Letters/Sounds/Rime Review	-ate, -ave, -ame
Words	mates, cake, saved
Sentence	Frank's mates lost the game.

Target Skills for Game Plan

The target skills for the Game Plan focus on introducing a new syllable type – vowel-consonant-e (split vowel spelling words). The long vowels covered in the current chapter and Game Plans require a "cognitive flexing" of sorts due to the shift in vowel pronunciation. Until now, letters and their sounds have been connected through "paired associate learning", in which each letter has its "matching" sound. With the split vowel spelling syllable, pupils have to expand their associations to incorporate alternate sounds. The process places an additional cognitive burden on the reader. Pupils who demonstrated fluent word recognition with short vowel words are likely to cycle back to the Full Alphabetic/Decoding Phase when learning a new syllable type. Along these lines, there are three target skills for the current Game Plan, which lay the foundation for enhancing orthographic mapping and increasing overall reading fluency with complex texts.

- Reading split vowel spelling words
- Rules for spelling split vowel spelling words
- The drop 'e' rule for spelling split vowel spelling words with suffixes/inflectional endings

Your Team

Pupils are ready for this type of instruction when they can accurately read single- and multi-syllable words with short vowel sounds (e.g. sun, pot, napkin, picnic). These include longer words with digraphs or adjacent consonants in either the initial or final position (e.g. shin, punch, sting). Pupils at this phase demonstrate a basic ability to read and spell one- and two-syllable words with suffixes -s, -es and -ing (e.g. flats, dishes, trumpets, hitting, lunchboxes). They also may have been introduced to decoding and encoding single-syllable split vowel spelling words (e.g. shine, crane, drove).

Case Study

Lee is a Year 1 pupil with solid skills reading one- and two-syllable short vowel words. Lee readily moved from the letters and sound phase to connected phonation, and then, using backwards decoding, developed accuracy and automaticity with single and short vowel words. Lee regularly uses strategies such as syllable division and backwards decoding to aid him in fluently reading words with two closed syllables. However, Lee reverts to sound-by-sound decoding for split vowel spelling syllable type words. What strategies can help Lee become accurate and automatic reading and spelling split vowel spelling syllable type words?

Your Equipment

Series: Dandelion Readers Split Vowel Spellings (ISBN 9781907170270)

Reader: *Late* (Book 1)

Phonics Concept: Rime pattern recognition of split vowel spelling words; closed/split vowel spelling syllable division; drop 'e'.

Book Overview:
Frank's chronic tardiness causes many problems, but luckily his mum offers a great solution.

Text from the Book *Late*

Frank was late.

He was late for school.

He did not wake up in the morning.

Frank was late for Dad's birthday!

"Shame!" said Mum. "No cake left on the plate."

Then Frank was late for the football game.

His team lost the game.

His mates blamed him.

Beth was red in the face.

"Take this!" She gave him a box. "Don't be late for the next game!"

Frank looked in the box. A clock!

The next day, Frank was not late for the game!

Frank saved a goal!

His mates yelled, "Frank saved the day!"

Frank was never late again.

Additional Texts

The Phonic Books series simultaneously introduces the split vowel spelling syllable in single- and multi-syllable words. For some pupils, it may be necessary to introduce and practise single-syllable words with the split vowel spelling pattern before attempting mixed practice. In the **Dandelion Readers Split Vowel Spellings** series, Book 1 introduces 'a-e', pronounced with the long sound of /ae/ (also depicted as /ai/, /ā/ or /A/), Book 2 introduces 'e-e', pronounced with the long sound of /ee/ (also depicted as /ē/ or /E/), Book 3 introduces 'i-e', pronounced with the long sound of /ie/ (also depicted as /ī/ or /I/), Book 4 introduces 'o-e', pronounced with the long sound of /oe/ (also depicted as /ō/ or /O/) and Book 5 introduces 'u-e', pronounced with the long sound of /ue/ (also depicted as /oo/, /ū/ or /U/). Book 6 reviews all split vowel spelling patterns. **Dandelion World Split Vowel Spellings** (ISBN 9780241699843) is another series that covers the same phonics focus using non-fiction texts.

Planning for Game Day

Similar to all the Game Plans in the book, this lesson was designed using a backwards planning approach. By utilising a backwards planning approach, all skill development activities are aligned with patterns, vocabulary and text that pupils encounter in the accompanying book. Backwards planning ensures that lessons are tightly focused on building and applying a cohesive set of skills. The sequence for backwards planning is shared in the following breakout box.

Backwards Planning Using a Decodable Text

Planning Reading Activities (Sentences, Single Words, RAN Charts, Letter Sounds and Suffix Review)

Step 1: Choose three sentences from the text. Select sentences that offer practice for target phonics skills.

Step 2: Select four individual words that appear in the sentences for single word reading practice.

Step 3: Use the individual words and phrases from the sentences to create your RAN charts.

Step 4: Choose starters or rime patterns to teach sound-symbol correspondence.

Step 5: Review the spelling, pronunciation and meaning of relevant suffixes.

Planning Heart Word and Dictation Activity

Step 1: Choose up to four heart words/ irregular words from the text.

Step 2: Select rime patterns, one heart word, three single words and at least one sentence from the reading activities for dictation tasks.

Planning Vocabulary and Comprehension Activities

Step 1: Choose one multiple-meaning vocabulary word from the book for instruction.

Step 2: Read the story and craft questions that require pupils to find the information in the text (factual questions), analyse word meaning (semantic questions) or "read between the lines" to understand the deeper purpose of the story (inference questions). Set a purpose for reading by providing a question for pupils to keep in mind as they read the book.

Winning Strategies

The instructional routines in the Game Plan support developing pupils' ability to accurately read and spell split vowel spelling words. Instruction also supports encoding development by teaching spelling rules for split vowel spelling words with suffixes. The Winning Strategies in this chapter include:

- Backwards decoding split vowel spelling words
- Decoding multisyllabic words with short and long vowel sounds
- Spelling split vowel spelling words with suffixes using the drop 'e' rule

Backwards Decoding Single-Syllable Split Vowel Spelling Words

Teachers can support pupils' efficiency in word recognition by reinforcing the use of backwards decoding with single-syllable split vowel spelling words. Similar to the backwards decoding instruction in Chapters 2–6, pupils are guided to read the rime pattern prior to the starter sound and then pronounce the whole word. This approach is especially effective for the split vowel spelling pattern because attention is drawn to the final silent 'e' early in the reading process. For example, the word "snake" is read "-ake", "sn-", "snake". Although counterintuitive to some who insist that words are always processed left to right, backwards decoding serves to break words into larger chunks, activate pupils' auditory memory for similar words and support accurate pronunciation of the vowel. Together these processes facilitate efficient orthographic mapping and support the transition from decoding to sight word recognition. See Chapter 2 (page 43) for a review of the evidence supporting backwards decoding.

Decoding Multisyllabic Words with Closed and Split Vowel Spelling Syllables

When words contain multiple syllables, pupils require a strategic approach for systematically dividing them into larger chunks and efficiently pronouncing each syllable. Most multisyllabic words can be decoded with a few key division strategies. These approaches break the word into small digestible units or letter patterns. Teaching and practising syllable division methods ensures that pupils have a strategic approach as they encounter longer and/or unknown words. See Chapter 5 (page 117) for a review of the importance of syllable division strategies.

Spelling Split Vowel Spelling Words with Suffixes Using the Drop 'e' Rule

Instruction on the spelling rules for adding suffixes to split vowel spelling words offers important reading and writing support for pupils. The process of adding suffixes to split vowel spelling words is best described by the drop 'e' rule, which requires the elimination of the final silent 'e' during the spelling process (e.g. like + ing = liking, save + ed = saved). As a reminder, no change occurs to the base word when spelling with suffix -s; writers can just add the suffix and carry on.

Step 1: Teach Phonics Concepts Using Winning Strategies

Three target phonics skills are featured in the current Game Plan. The first skill is developing accuracy and automaticity reading split vowel spelling words using the backwards decoding approach. The additional phonics skills are taught during the dictation portion of the lesson.

WINNING STRATEGY: Backwards Decoding Split Vowel Spelling Words

As described in Chapter 5, English words are composed of syllables. A syllable is a word or part of a word with one vowel sound. There are six syllable types in English. Pupils have already learnt closed syllable words in which the vowel sound is short and closed in by a consonant. In the current Game Plan, pupils will practise their skills with a new syllable type, split vowel spelling words (also known as silent 'e' or vowel-consonant-e words). Split vowel spelling words are characterised by a long vowel sound and a final silent 'e'. Practising the pronunciation of the vowel in single-syllable split vowel spelling words offers pupils an opportunity to create a strong association between vowels and their new associated sounds.

Step-by-Step Instruction for Backwards Decoding

The backwards decoding strategy helps pupils process the entire word during reading, correctly pronounce the vowel sound and move towards automatic word recognition. In order to efficiently backwards decode, pupils must understand how to identify a rime pattern. This process is initially introduced in Chapter 2. Then, pupils are instructed to read the words from back to front, first reading the rime pattern, then pronouncing the starter sound in isolation and finally blending the sounds together to produce the entire word.

Teacher Script for Backwards Decoding Split Vowel Spelling Words

Introduction to Strategy

Teacher: *Today, we are going to use our backwards decoding strategy on a new syllable type. This syllable is called a vowel-consonant-e syllable because the sequence of letters in the rime pattern will be vowel, consonant, final silent 'e'. Let me demonstrate.*

Type of Word

One-Syllable Words with Split Vowel Spelling and Closed Syllables

Syllable Division for Single-Syllable Words

Write the first word, "rake".

Teacher: *Let's find and underline the rime pattern. In order to find the rime pattern, we have to find the vowel sound and the letters that follow.*

Run finger under the word and stop at 'a'.

Teacher: *Our rime pattern is A-K-E. Notice the final silent 'e' in the word.* (Point under final silent 'e'.)

Teacher: *The final silent 'e' makes the 'a' sound long – the rime pattern is "-ake". Your turn to say the rime pattern.* (Elicit "-ake".)

My turn to pronounce the starter sound – "r-". Your turn. (Elicit "r-".)

My turn to say the whole word – "rake". Your turn. (Elicit "rake".)

Additional Practice

wake **same** **plate** **flake**

Final Silent 'e' Is Booked and Busy

In split vowel spelling words, readers rely on the presence of final silent 'e' as the primary pronunciation cue. However, final silent 'e' has several jobs in English, and they all can impact the pronunciation of the vowel. The most prominent job is influencing the vowel pronunciation so that it is a "long sound". Approximately 50 per cent of words with final silent 'e' have long vowel sounds (Eide, 2012).

However, it can be helpful to let developing readers know that final silent 'e' has other jobs to do as well, such as preventing words from ending with the letters 'i', 'u' or 'v' (e.g. clu/clue) or providing clarity on the voicing of 'th' (e.g. teeth/teethe). It may not be necessary to offer in-depth instruction of each of the variants of final silent 'e', but when noticed by a pupil, a logical explanation can provide context for the spelling pattern.

WINNING STRATEGY: Decoding Multisyllabic Words with Short and Long Vowel Sounds

To accurately read multisyllabic words, most pupils follow a set of sequential strategies. The strategy in this chapter builds on instruction from Chapter 5 (page 122), in which pupils are taught to identify vowel sounds, underline the associated rime patterns and divide the syllables between the rime patterns. The same practice is followed here. Once the word is accurately divided, correctly pronounce the syllables using decoding. Read the last syllable first. Finally, reread the whole word as one unit.

Teacher Script for Dividing Multisyllabic Words with Split Vowel Spelling and Closed Syllables

Introduction to Strategy

Teacher: *Let's continue breaking up our words by syllable. You might notice two different types of syllables in these words – split vowel spelling and closed syllables. We will read our words using the backwards decoding technique.*

Type of Word

Two-Syllable Words with Split Vowel Spelling and Closed Syllables

Syllable Division for Multisyllabic Words

Write the first word, "reptile".

Teacher: *First, I am going to find the letters making vowel sounds and put dots underneath.* (Run finger under the word and put dots under the first 'e' and the 'i'.)

Teacher: *We have found our two vowel sounds* (indicate dots), *so we know this is a two-syllable word. Notice that I did not put a dot under the final silent 'e' because it is not making a vowel sound. The dot also indicates where our rime pattern begins. Let's underline our rime patterns.* (Underline the following patterns: reptile.)

Teacher: *Now we are ready to divide our word into individual syllables. We will divide after our rime patterns.* (Divide as follows: rep·tile.)

Teacher: *Let's backwards decode the word, starting with the last syllable. Remember that this is our new syllable, split vowel spelling, so be careful of that vowel sound – "tile". Your turn.* (Elicit "tile".)

First syllable is "rep". Your turn. (Elicit "rep".)

The whole word is "reptile". Your turn. (Elicit "reptile".)

Step 2: Reinforce Letters/Sounds in Isolation

The Game Plan features four split vowel spelling rime patterns and two closed syllable rime patterns featured in the story *Late*. The focus on rime patterns is intended to ensure that pupils are not only accurate with vowel sound pronunciation but can also blend the vowels with consonant sounds that are common in syllable chunks.

Letter/Sound Review for Game Plan

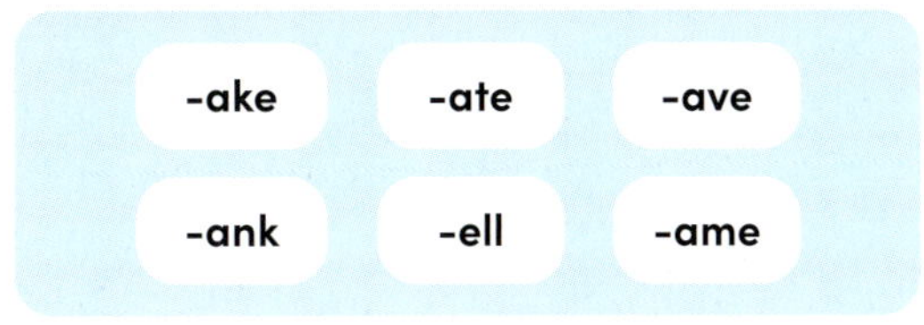

Step 3: Suffix Review

The Game Plan incorporates a review of previously taught suffixes. During the review, instruction elicits pupils' knowledge of suffix spelling, purpose and varied pronunciations. In the current lesson, pupils will review previously taught suffixes -ed, -s and -ing.

Starting in Chapter 4, suffixes are initially introduced by explicitly teaching the spelling, pronunciation and purpose of the suffix. There are no new suffixes taught in the current chapter, but suffixes are present throughout the texts, and a review is always helpful. See the **Teacher Script to Review Suffixes -ed, -es and -ing** on page 170.

Suffixes for Game Plan

-ed | -s | -ing

Step 4: Apply Phonics Concept to Single Words from the Text

The lesson's keywords serve as a platform for practising target phonics and morphology skills. The Game Plan features four words from the text *Late*. Each word is relevant to the target reading skill of decoding split vowel spelling words, including those with affixes.

Individual Words for Game Plan

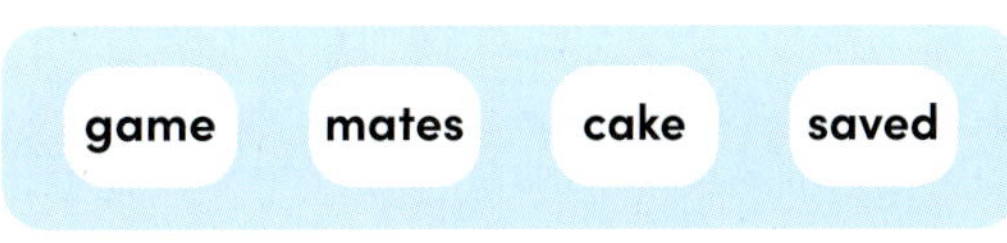

Teacher Script to Review Suffixes -ed, -es and -ing

Introduction to Strategy

Teacher: *Let's quickly review the suffixes we already know.*

I will say the suffix is spelt _____. It changes the base word by _____ and is pronounced _____.

Language for Reviewing Suffix -ed

Write "-ed" on the board.

Teacher: *This suffix is spelt ________.* (Elicit correct spelling.)

Teacher: *Suffix -ed changes the base word in one way.*

1. *It puts a verb into the _____ tense.* (Elicit "past".)

Teacher: *Suffix -ed has three pronunciations.*

1. *When words end in 'd' or 't', suffix -ed is pronounced ______.* (Elicit /ed/.)

2. *When words end in voiced sounds, suffix -ed is pronounced ______.* (Elicit /d/.)

3. *When words end in unvoiced sounds, suffix -ed is pronounced ______.* (Elicit /t/.)

Language for Reviewing Suffix -es

Write "-es" on the board.

Teacher: *This suffix is spelt ________.* (Elicit correct spelling.)

Teacher: *Suffix -es changes the base word in two ways.*

1. *It makes a noun _____.* (Elicit "plural".)

2. *It puts a verb in the present __________.* (Elicit "tense".)

Teacher: *Suffix -es is pronounced _______.* (Elicit /ez/.)

Language for Reviewing Suffix -ing

Write "-ing" on the board.

Teacher: *This suffix is spelt ________.* (Elicit correct spelling.)

Teacher: *Suffix -ing changes a verb to make the action __________.* (Elicit "happen continuously".)

Teacher: *Suffix -ing is pronounced ______.* (Elicit /ing/.)

Step-by-Step Practice Reading Split Vowel Spelling Words with Suffixes

After teaching pupils the pronunciation of long vowel sounds and introducing them to split vowel spelling syllables, it is helpful to include activities that ensure accurate and automatic word reading. Some pupils are able to apply their knowledge of split vowel spelling patterns seamlessly. Others require a structured or scaffolded approach that guides them through backwards decoding the base word, pronouncing the suffix in isolation and rereading the whole word. A scaffolded approach is demonstrated in the **Teacher Script for Backwards Decoding Words by Base, Affix and in Combined Form**. Although this step may be unnecessary for some, it can be a helpful tool, as the spellings of many base words are impacted by the presence of a suffix. For example, in words where the final letter is dropped (e.g. tape/taped), a visual that depicts the original base word (tape) and the compounded form (taped) reminds pupils that even when spellings shift, pronunciation remains the same.

Teacher Script for Backwards Decoding Words by Base, Affix and in Combined Form

Introduction to Strategy

Teacher: *Let's practise reading split vowel spelling words with our new strategy. I will backwards decode the base word, pronounce the suffix (if there is one) and then combine them into the complete word.*

Gradual Release Model	Base Word	Backwards Decode	Suffix	Complete Word
Teacher Models	game	/ame/ + /g/ = /game/		game
Teacher and Pupils Together	mate	/ate/ + /m/ = /mate/	-s	mates
Pupils Alone	cake	/ake/ + /k/ = /cake/		cake
Pupils Alone	save	/ave/ + /s/ = /save/	-ed	saved

Step 5: Build Knowledge of Irregular/Heart Words

The Game Plan has four selected heart words from the text *Late*. Two of the words are permanently irregular ("said" and "the") and two of the words are temporarily irregular ("school" and "was") because it is assumed pupils have not yet been taught the phonics patterns. Educators can use their discretion about whether or not to teach a temporarily irregular word using the same protocol as for a permanently irregular word. Below, these words are segmented by their sounds. The sound-symbol correspondence is presented, and any irregular spellings are noted with a heart below the letter pattern. The heart word instruction strategy is initially introduced, and a teacher script provided, in Chapter 2 (pages 51–53).

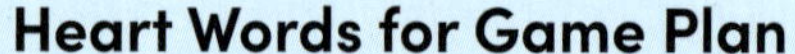

Heart Words for Game Plan

Sound 1	Sound 2	Sound 3	Sound 4
/s/	/k/	/oo/	/l/
s	**ch**	**oo**	l

said

Sound 1	Sound 2	Sound 3
/s/	/e/	/d/
s	**ai**	d

Sound 1	Sound 2
/th/	/u/
th	**e**

Sound 1	Sound 2	Sound 3
/w/	/u/	/z/
w	**a**	s

Step 6: Enhance Sight Word Recognition with RAN Charts

Individual words and phrases from the text *Late* are used for the RAN charts. RAN charts are highlighted in Chapter 3 as a Winning Strategy and serve as a platform to practise automatic retrieval of single words and phrases. To maximise participation for all pupils, RAN charts should be read chorally, with pupils first reading the word or phrase in their head before reading as a pair or group.

RAN Charts for Game Plan

lost the game	saved the day	his mates	no cake left
his mates	lost the game	no cake left	lost the game
saved the day	no cake left	lost the game	his mates
no cake left	lost the game	his mates	saved the day

game	mates	cake	saved
cake	game	saved	mates
mates	saved	game	cake
saved	cake	saved	game

Step 7: Practise Reading Sentences from the Text

The sentence reading portion of the lesson offers pupils an opportunity to practise integrating decoding, heart word and sight word skills. By selecting a variety of sentences from the decodable text as a platform for practice, pupils are incrementally introduced to elements of the story. This routine allows pupils the chance to practise backwards decoding, sight word recognition and syntactic phrasing.

Syntactic phrasing is a strategy that involves teaching pupils to recognise and group words into phrases based on the syntax, or structure, of sentences. This approach supports the development of both fluency and comprehension by enabling readers to process text in manageable chunks, rather than reading the sentence word by word. See Chapter 6 (page 151) for more information about syntactic phrasing. Refer to the **Teacher Script for Syntactic Phrasing During Sentence Reading** on page 175 for a demonstration of how to integrate syntactic phrasing into the lesson's sentence reading activities.

Sentences for Game Plan

His team lost the game.

Frank was not late for the game!

Frank's mates yelled, "Frank saved the day!"

Punctuation Provides Clues to Prosody

Punctuation provides readers with a visual guide to written text. The use of full stops and commas, as well as exclamation, question and quotation marks, indicates where pauses, pitch changes and intonation should occur when reading aloud. Different punctuation marks indicate varying lengths of pauses, with a comma signifying a slightly shorter pause than a full stop and a question mark suggesting a rising pitch at the end of a sentence. Further, punctuation also plays a role in clarifying meaning. In the famous example sentence, "Let's eat Grandma", the missing comma dramatically changes the sentence from the intended meaning that it is time to eat ("Let's eat, Grandma."). Reviewing the symbols and purpose of key punctuation is helpful for supporting pupils' automaticity and comprehension.

Teacher Script for Syntactic Phrasing During Sentence Reading

Introduction to Strategy

Teacher: *We are going to read some sentences. First, we are going to read the sentence quietly, then I will show you how to break it up into phrases. Next, we will practise reading the phrases. Finally, I will ask you some comprehension questions about the sentence.*

Introduce Purpose and Approach to Syntactic Phrasing

Write or project the sentence: Frank's mates yelled, "Frank saved the day!"

Teacher: *First, I would like you to read the sentence quietly.*

Elicit silent reading from pupils.

Teacher: *Now, watch me break up the sentence into phrases.*

Scoop underneath the phrases shown below to break up the sentence. Describe the type of phrase as necessary.

Teacher: *Please copy the phrase scoops onto your sheet. It's your turn to read as a group.*

Pupils chorally read aloud, following the teacher's pointer/finger as each phrase is scooped.

Teacher: *I have a few questions to ask you about this sentence.*

Use the following prompts as appropriate:

Who is this sentence about? (Subject phrase.)

What happened to ________? (Predicate phrase.)

Where, when or how did it happen? (Prepositional phrase.)

Did anything else happen to the subject? (For compound sentences.)

What are you picturing in your mind? (Visualisation strategy.)

Repeat steps as appropriate for remaining sentences.

Additional Practice

A suggested syntactic structure for additional sentences is offered below. Sentences may be simplified or modified for this activity.

Frank's team	lost	the game.
Subject	**Verb**	**Object**

Frank	was not late	for the game!
Subject	**Verb Phrase**	**Prepositional Phrase**

Step 8: Expand Text-Related Vocabulary Knowledge

Activating pupils' knowledge of multiple-meaning words from the text supports the development of their word recognition skills. The word "game" was chosen as the multiple-meaning word for the current lesson. As in Chapters 4, 5 and 6, instruction deepens pupils' understanding of word meanings by providing child-friendly definitions and associations as well as illustrations of meaning.

Vocabulary Word for Game Plan

Vocabulary Term
game
Pupil-Friendly Definition 1
An activity or sport where you follow rules and try to win. (noun)
Using the Term in a Sentence
Her football game was postponed due to bad weather.
Pupil-Friendly Definition 2
You are willing to try something new. (adjective)
Using the Term in a Sentence
He said he was game for a road trip to a new place.
Questions for Discussion

- What kinds of games do people play?
- When playing a game, what are some things you might need?
- Where do people play games?
- What are some things that you might be game to do?

Step 9: Putting It All Together for Text Reading and Comprehension

The following questions have been generated for the current Game Plan and the text *Late*. See Chapter 1 (pages 29 and 32) for guidance on engaging strategies for reading aloud, including the use of choral reading.

Comprehension Questions for Game Plan

Factual
What is a problematic pattern for Frank?

Inferential
Why did Frank receive an alarm clock from Beth?

Vocabulary in Context
At the end of the story, Frank's pals say he "saved the day". About what other character in the story could this term be used?

Text from the Book *Late*

Frank was late.

He was late for school.

He did not wake up in the morning.

Frank was late for Dad's birthday!

"Shame!" said Mum. "No cake left on the plate."

Then Frank was late for the football game.

His team lost the game.

His mates blamed him.

Beth was red in the face.

"Take this!" She gave him a box. "Don't be late for the next game!"

Frank looked in the box. A clock!

The next day, Frank was not late for the game!

Frank saved a goal!

His mates yelled, "Frank saved the day!"

Frank was never late again.

Step 10: Applying Phonics Knowledge to Dictation

Pupils benefit from a comprehensive approach that simultaneously supports the development of phonics skills for both word reading and spelling. Therefore, a selection of sounds, words and sentences used for reading have been featured in the dictation portion of the Game Plan. The dictation activity provides an opportunity to reinforce spelling of single-syllable split vowel spelling words and the strategy for adding suffixes to split vowel spelling words.

Dictation Routine for Game Plan

Dictation	Selected Elements
Heart Word	school
Letters/Rime Patterns	-ate, -ave, -ame
Words	mates, cake, saved
Sentence	Frank's team lost the game.

WINNING STRATEGY: Spelling Split Vowel Spelling Words with Suffixes Using the Drop 'e' Rule

Similar to the suffix spelling strategies introduced in Chapter 6, it is important for pupils to consider the pattern of the base word before adding a suffix. As a general rule, spelling changes occur to the base word in order to preserve the original syllable type and pronunciation of the vowel. The drop 'e' rule provides pupils with a strategic approach for adding a suffix to single-syllable or multi-syllable words ending with final silent 'e'.

Step-by-Step Instruction for the Drop 'e' Rule

The drop 'e' rule cues the reader to pronounce the base word's vowel as a long sound. One effective way for teaching the drop 'e' rule is to prompt pupils with a series of questions.

1. Does the base word end in a final silent 'e'?
2. Does the suffix begin with a vowel?

If the answer to both questions is yes, drop the final silent 'e' before adding the suffix. If the answer to either question is no, do not drop the 'e' before adding the suffix. See the **Teacher Script to Practise Drop 'e'** and the **Teacher Script for Prompted Strategies During Dictation** on page 179 for suggested teacher language.

Practising spelling split vowel spelling words with suffixes is a productive activity that should occur either the day before the traditional dictation exercise or directly precede it. When delivering this activity, it is helpful to scaffold the spelling conversation.

Teacher Script to Practise Drop 'e'

Instruction	Teacher Models	Teacher and Pupils Together	Pupils Alone	Pupils Alone	Pupils Alone
Present base word	*Let's add "-ed" to the word "flake".*	*Let's add "-ed" to the word "cave".*	*Let's add "-s" to the word "plate".*	*Let's add "-ing" to the word "make".*	*Let's add "-ing" to the word "race".*
Model "think aloud" for drop 'e' rule	*Does the base word have a final silent 'e'?* (yes) *Does the suffix begin with a vowel?* (yes)	*Does the base word have a final silent 'e'?* (yes) *Does the suffix begin with a vowel?* (yes)	*Does the base word have a final silent 'e'?* (yes) *Does the suffix begin with a vowel?* (no)	*Does the base word have a final silent 'e'?* (yes) *Does the suffix begin with a vowel?* (yes)	*Does the base word have a final silent 'e'?* (yes) *Does the suffix begin with a vowel?* (yes)
What is the drop 'e' rule?	*Yes, drop the final silent 'e' – "flaked".*	*Yes, drop the final silent 'e' – "caved".*	*No, just add the 's' and carry on – "plates".*	*Yes, drop the final silent 'e' – "making".*	*Yes, drop the final silent 'e' – "racing".*

Teacher Script for Prompted Strategies During Dictation

Spelling Words with Suffixes

Teacher: *Your word to spell is ________.* (saved)

Pupils repeat the word.

Teacher: *This is a word with the suffix -ed. Let's spell and write our base word first. For words with final silent 'e', ask these questions:*

1. Does the base word have a final silent 'e'?
2. Does the suffix begin with a vowel?

Teacher: *If the answer to both questions is yes, drop the 'e' before adding the suffix.*

Teacher: *The word to spell is ________.* (mates)

Pupils repeat the word.

Teacher: *This is a word with the suffix -s. Let's spell and write our base word first. For words with final silent 'e', ask these questions:*

1. Does the base word have a final silent 'e'?
2. Does the suffix begin with a vowel?

Teacher: *If both answers are yes, drop the 'e'. If the answer to one question is no, do not drop the 'e'.*

Proposed Practice Schedule

The Game Plan for this phase of word reading is broken into 10 steps. The plan has been broken up over the course of four days to keep sessions to 20 minutes or under. As always, when modifying the schedule, it is recommended that opportunities to apply skills to connected text are prioritised. Connected text practice has not been identified on Days 1 and 4. Teachers will want to identify appropriate texts to include on these days.

<table>
<tr><th colspan="2">Day 1 (20 mins)</th><th colspan="2">Day 2 (18 mins)</th><th>Day 3 (20 mins)</th><th>Day 4 (10 mins)</th></tr>
<tr><td rowspan="2">Phonics Concept (10 mins)</td><td rowspan="2">Suffix Review (3 mins)</td><td rowspan="2">RAN Chart – Single Words (3 mins)</td><td rowspan="2">Vocabulary (5 mins)</td><td>RAN Chart – Phrases (5 mins)</td><td rowspan="3">Dictation (10 mins)</td></tr>
<tr><td>Book Reading and Comprehension Questions (5 mins)</td></tr>
<tr><td>Letter Sounds for Rime Patterns (2 mins)</td><td>Single Words (5 mins)</td><td>Heart Words (5 mins)</td><td>Sentences (5 mins)</td><td>Introduce and Practise with Drop 'e' (10 mins)</td></tr>
</table>

Game Plan

Decodable Text: ***Pete*, Dandelion Readers Split Vowel Spellings, Book 2**
Phonics Concept: **Rime pattern recognition of split vowel spelling words; closed/split vowel spelling syllable division; drop 'e'**

Letter/Sound/Rime Review			Phonics Concept
-ete	-ese	-ask	Provide direct instruction in the phonics concept, utilising words pulled from the Reader and/or that fit the patterns you are teaching.
-ess	-ash	-ish	

Suffix Review

-ed	-es	-s

Single Word Reading

completed	delete	concrete	these

Heart Words

began	is	to	said

RAN Charts (Single Words and Phrases)

completed	delete	concrete	these	completed his task	on the concrete	pressed delete	these dishes
delete	completed	these	concrete	pressed delete	completed his task	these dishes	on the concrete
concrete	these	completed	delete	on the concrete	these dishes	completed his task	pressed delete
these	delete	concrete	completed	these dishes	pressed delete	on the concrete	completed his task

Sentence Reading

Dad completed his task.

The milk bottles smashed onto the concrete.

Dad had to press the 'delete' button to stop him.

Multiple-Meaning Word: concrete

Definition 1	Definition 2	Questions
(n) A liquid substance used for building that hardens quickly.	(adj) Something that is specific and real.	What does it mean to have concrete plans? What are some things that concrete is used to build?
Sentence 1 The truck arrived to pour the concrete for the house's foundation.	**Sentence 2** We need concrete evidence that you are working on the project.	

Story and Comprehension Questions

What happens when Pete tries to help Mum?	How did Mum feel in the end?	Why does the author write "snapped Mum", instead of "said Mum"?

Dictation

Heart Word	onto
Letters/Sounds/Rime Patterns	-ete, -ask, -ish
Words	complete, these, delete
Sentence	The milk bottles smashed onto the concrete.

In practice, RAN phrases should be displayed across a single line.

Glossary

Auditory memory The ability to take in, process, store and recall orally presented information

Automaticity The ability to effortlessly read words without having to decode them

Backwards decoding Decoding a syllable by the rime unit before the onset (e.g. reading "-ake", then "fl-", then saying "flake")

Backwards planning A strategic approach to instruction that involves starting with the desired outcome and working backwards to identify the steps or skills needed to reach the goal

Choral reading A technique where all pupils in the group (or class) read in unison in order to optimise opportunities for practice

Closed syllable A syllable that ends with a consonant rather than a vowel

Consolidated Alphabetic Phase One of Linnea Ehri's phases of word reading where pupils develop the ability to automatically pronounce entire words without decoding

Consonant A speech sound that is produced by obstructing the airflow in the vocal tract

Consonant digraph Two consonants that work together to represent a single sound (phoneme) (e.g. sh, th, ch, etc.)

Context processor The part of the brain that uses surrounding information to confirm meaning (Four-Part Processing Model)

Continuous blending An instructional technique for sounding out words without pausing between sounds (sometimes called connected phonation)

Continuous sound A sound (phoneme) that can be elongated without becoming distorted; all vowels are continuous sounds, as well as some consonants, including 's' and 'm'

Decodable text Highly controlled reading material that aligns with phonics skills pupils have been taught, allowing pupils to decode, or sound out, words to practise skills in connected text

Decoding The process of using letter-sound knowledge to blend sounds together to read words

Dictation A teaching technique where teachers say sounds, words or sentences aloud and pupils demonstrate knowledge by writing the appropriate sound, word or sentence

Encoding Using knowledge of sounds (phonemes) to spell words

Explicit instruction A structured, teacher-led approach involving step-by-step directions, demonstration and plentiful practice opportunities

Fluency A reading behaviour that indicates a reader is automatic across all aspects of word knowledge; characterised by prosodic and effortless reading so energy can be dedicated to understanding content/meaning

Four-Part Processing Model A model of how the brain learns to read, highlighting the interactive nature of multiple aspects of language knowledge, including phonological, orthographic, semantic and context in reading development

Full Alphabetic Phase One of Linnea Ehri's phases of word reading where pupils attend to every letter in a word and have an understanding of the sound-symbol relationship in order to convert letters into sounds and blend to pronounce words

Grapheme-phoneme correspondence The relationship between letters and their corresponding sounds (also known as sound-symbol or letter-sound correspondence)

Heart word High-frequency words that contain one or more irregular spelling patterns

High-frequency word The most commonly occurring words in text (e.g. the, of, and); high-frequency words may be considered irregular words or heart words

Meaning processor The part of the brain that connects words to their meanings (Four-Part Processing Model)

Morpheme The smallest unit of meaning in a word

Morphology The study of meaningful word parts (morphemes) and how they combine to form words

Onset The part of a syllable that precedes the vowel; onsets consist of one or more consonants

Orthographic mapping The mental process by which readers store written words and their spellings to long-term memory for instant recognition, enabling fluent reading

Orthographic processor The part of the brain that focuses on the visual patterns of letters and their combinations, allowing for identification of letters and words (Four-Part Processing Model)

Partial Alphabetic Phase One of Linnea Ehri's phases of word reading where pupils are just beginning to make grapheme-phoneme connections

Phonemic awareness The ability to hear, identify and manipulate individual sounds in words

Phonological awareness The ability to understand, recognise and manipulate spoken language, including words, syllables, onsets/rimes and phonemes; an essential early reading skill

Phonological processor The part of the brain responsible for recognising, processing and manipulating sounds in spoken language (Four-Part Processing Model)

Pre-Alphabetic Phase The first phase in Linnea Ehri's phases of word reading where children rely on visual cues, rather than grapheme-phoneme relationships, to recognise words

Prosody The rhythm, stress and intonation patterns in a spoken language that contribute to overall understanding

RAN chart Rapid Automatic Naming chart; a tool that provides a repeated presentation of single words or phrases from a text, offering the automatic retrieval of common single words and phrases

Reading circuit The network in the brain that allows for the connection of visual and linguistic processes

Rebellious rime patterns Closed syllables where the vowel makes the long sound rather than the expected short sound (sometimes called closed syllable exception words)

Rime pattern The part of a syllable that includes the vowel and any letters after it

Scarborough's Reading Rope A model illustrating the complex and interconnected skills involved in proficient reading; the reading rope depicts two intertwined strands, word recognition and language comprehension, which are both critical to developing fluent and meaningful reading

Scooping Grouping words in phrases

Segmenting Breaking words apart into individual phonemes; segmenting is a key part of phonemic awareness and is integral to the ability to decode and spell words

Semantic neighbourhood A group of words that have similar meanings or are connected in some way

Semantics The study of the meaning of words, phrases and sentences

Sight word Any words that are recognised and read automatically, meaning that they do not need to be sounded out, or decoded

Simple View of Reading A theory positing that reading comprehension is the result of two factors: decoding and language comprehension; weakness in one component will impact overall reading comprehension

Simultaneous Oral Spelling A multisensory method of teaching spelling that uses visual, auditory and kinaesthetic learning to spell words

Sound-symbol correspondence See Grapheme-phoneme correspondence

Starter sound The first part of a word or syllable that appears before the rime (e.g. /b/ in "bat", /sh/ in "ship"); the initial sound

Stop sound A consonant sound that is made by briefly blocking airflow and releasing it (e.g. /b/, /p/, /k/, /t/)

Structured Literacy An evidenced-based approach to teaching reading and spelling that provides explicit, systematic, cumulative and diagnostic instruction to develop foundational literacy skills

Suffix A word part added to the end of a base word that changes its meaning or grammatical function

Syllable A word or part of a word with one vowel sound

Syntactic phrasing Grouping words into meaningful phrases while reading in order to support understanding

Syntax The set of rules that governs how words, phrases and clauses are arranged to form clear and meaningful sentences

Unvoiced sounds Speech sounds that are produced without the vibration of vocal cords (e.g. /f/, /k/, /p/, /t/, /s/)

Visual word form area Also known as the brain's "letterbox", this area of the brain is specialised for recognition of letters, letter strings and words and interacts with other language-related areas of the brain as part of the reading circuit

Voiced sounds Speech sounds that are produced with the vibration of the vocal cords (e.g. /b/, /d/, /g/, /v/, /z/)

Vowel A speech sound produced without blocking the airflow

Index

Acknowledgments

R. C. Anderson et al, *Becoming a nation of readers: The report of the Commission on Reading*, National Institute of Education, 1985. (page 15)

J. M. Anglin, G. A. Miller and P. C. Wakefield, "Vocabulary development: A morphological analysis," *Monographs of the Society for Research in Child Development*, 58 (10), 1993. (pages 91, 117)

A. L. Archer and C. A. Hughes, *Explicit Instruction: Effective and Efficient Teaching*, Guilford Press, 2011. (pages 7–8, 29, 36, 62)

I. L. Beck, M. G. McKeown and L. Kucan, *Bringing Words to Life: Robust Vocabulary Instruction*, Guilford Press, 2013. (pages 12, 83, 106)

C. F. A. Benjamin and N. Gaab, "What's the story? The tale of reading fluency told at speed," *Human Brain Mapping*, 33 (11), 2012. (page 9)

B. A. Blachman et al, *Road to the Code: A Phonological Awareness Program for Young Children*, Brookes Publishing Co., 2000. (page 33)

L. Buchanan, C. Burgess and K. Lund, "Overcrowding in semantic neighborhoods: Modelling deep dyslexia," *Brain and Cognition*, 32 (2), 1996. (pages 12, 81)

S. J. Carrier, "Effective strategies for teaching science vocabulary," LEARN North Carolina: UNC-Chapel Hill, NC, 2011. (page 92)

S . Dehaene, *Reading in the Brain: The New Science of How We Read*, Penguin, 2010. (page 9)

Department for Education, "Early years foundation stage profile handbook," 2024. Available at: https://www.gov.uk/government/publications/early-years-foundation-stage-profile-handbook (page 67)

Department for Education, "England moves to fourth in international rankings for reading," Department for Education, 2023. Available at: https://www.gov.uk/government/news/england-moves-to-fourth-in-international-rankings-for-reading (page 7)

R. E. Donegan and J. Wanzek, "Effects of reading interventions implemented for upper elementary struggling readers: A look at recent research," *Reading and Writing*, 34 (8), 2021. (pages 7–8)

N. K. Duke et al, "Authentic literacy activities for developing comprehension and writing," *The Reading Teacher*, 60 (4), 2006. (page 15)

L. C. Ehri, "Learning to read words: Theory, findings, and issues," *Scientific Studies of Reading*, 9 (2), 2005. (page 30)

L. C. Ehri, "Orthographic Mapping in the Acquisition of Sight Word Reading, Spelling Memory, and Vocabulary Learning," *Scientific Studies of Reading*, 18 (1), 2014.

L. C. Ehri, "Phases of development in learning to read words by sight," *Journal of Research in Reading*, 18 (2), 1995. (page 10)

D. Eide, *Uncovering the Logic of English: A Common-Sense Approach to Reading, Spelling, and Literacy*, Pedia Learning Inc., 2012. (pages 118, 167)

J. M. Fletcher et al, *Learning Disabilities: From Identification to Intervention*, Guilford Press, 2018. (page 7)

B. Foorman et al, "Foundational Skills to Support Reading for Understanding in Kindergarten through 3rd Grade." (NCEE 2016-4008), Washington, DC: National Center for Education Evaluation and Regional Assistance, Institute of Education Sciences, U.S. Department of Education, 2016. Available at: http://whatworks.ed.gov (page 7)

K. Galuschka et al, "Effectiveness of spelling interventions for learners with dyslexia: A meta-analysis and systematic review," *Educational Psychologist*, 55 (1), 2020. (page 44)

R. Gersten et al, "Assisting students struggling with reading: Response to Intervention and multi-tier intervention for reading in the primary grades. A practice guide" (NCEE 2009-4045), Washington, DC: National Center for Education Evaluation and Regional Assistance, Institute of Education Sciences, U.S. Department of Education, 2008. Available at: https://ies.ed.gov/ncee/wwc/practiceguides (page 15)

R. Gersten et al, "Meta-analysis of the impact of reading interventions for students in the primary grades," *Journal of Research on Educational Effectiveness*, 13 (2), 2020. (page 7)

S. M. Gonzalez-Frey and L. C. Ehri, "Connected phonation is more effective than segmented phonation for teaching beginning readers to decode unfamiliar words," *Scientific Studies of Reading*, 25 (3), 2021. (page 23)

P. B. Gough and W. E. Tunmer, "Decoding, reading, and reading disability," *RASE: Remedial and Special Education*, 7 (1), 1986. (pages 9, 30, 54)

S. Graham, "The sciences of reading and writing must become more fully integrated," *Reading Research Quarterly*, 55 (S1), 2020. (page 84)

S. Graham and T. Santangelo, "Does spelling instruction make students better spellers, readers, and writers? A meta-analytic review," *Reading and Writing*, 27 (9), 2014. (page 44)

S. Graham, K. R. Harris and B. F. Chorzempa, "Contribution of spelling instruction to the spelling, writing, and reading of poor spellers," *Journal of Educational Psychology*, 94 (4), 2002. (page 58)

R. Green, "Bridging the north-south literacy divide," *The Mill*, 2025. Available at: https://manchestermill.co.uk/bridging-the-north-south-literacy/ (page 6)

A. K. Hudson et al, "Elementary teachers' knowledge of foundational literacy skills: A critical piece of the puzzle in the science of reading," *Reading Research Quarterly*, 56 (S1), 2021. (page 6)

D. A. Kilpatrick, *Essentials of Assessing, Preventing, and Overcoming Reading Difficulties*, John Wiley & Sons, 2015. (page 43)

D. A. Kilpatrick, *Equipped for Reading Success: A Comprehensive, Step-by-Step Program for Developing Phoneme Awareness and Fluent Word Recognition*, Casey & Kirsch Publishers, 2020. (pages 10–11, 44, 46, 102, 117)

M. R. Kuhn, "What's Really Wrong with Round Robin Reading?," International Literacy Association, *Literacy Now*, 2014. Available at: https://www.literacyworldwide.org/blog/literacy-now/2014/05/07/what%27s-really-wrong-with-round-robin-reading- (page 33)

J. B. Lindsey, *Reading Above the Fray: Reliable, Research-Based Routines for Developing Decoding Skills*, Scholastic, 2022. (page 15)

M. W. Lovett et al, "Development and evaluation of a research-based intervention program for children and adolescents with reading disabilities," *Perspectives on Language and Literacy*, 40 (3), 2014. (pages 7–8)

B. D. McCandliss, L. Cohen and S. Dehaene, "The visual word form area: Expertise for reading in the fusiform gyrus," *Trends in Cognitive Sciences*, 7 (7), 2003. (page 20)

D. Mewhort and A. Beal, "Mechanisms of word identification," *Journal of Experimental Psychology: Human Perception and Performance*, 3 (4), 1977. (page 118)

L. C. Moats, "Teaching reading is rocket science: What expert teachers of reading should know and be able to do," *American Educator*, 44 (2), 2020. (pages 7, 58)

L. C. Moats and S. Brady, *Speech to Print: Language essentials for Teachers*, Paul H. Brookes Publishing Company, 2000. (pages 23, 33)

K. C. Moats and C. Tolman, "Module 3: Spellography for Teachers: How English Spelling Works", excerpted from *Language Essentials for Teachers of Reading and Spelling (LETRS)*, Boston: Sopris West, 2009. (page 58)

K. Mokhtari and H. B. Thompson, "How problems of reading fluency and comprehension are related to difficulties in syntactic awareness skills among fifth graders," *Literacy Research and Instruction*, 46 (1), 2006. (page 142)

R. D. Morris et al, "Multiple-component remediation for developmental reading disabilities: IQ, socioeconomic status, and race as factors in remedial outcome," *Journal of Learning Disabilities*, 45 (2), 2012. (pages 7–8)

K. Nation and M. J. Snowling, "Factors influencing syntactic awareness skills in normal readers and poor comprehenders," *Applied Psycholinguistics*, 21 (2), 2000. (page 142)

National Literacy Trust, "Key findings & summary," *National Literacy Trust*, 2025. Available at: https://literacytrust.org.uk/information/what-is-literacy/covid-19-and-literacy/key-findings-summary/ (page 6)

National Reading Panel (US), "Teaching children to read: An evidence-based assessment of the scientific research literature on reading and its implications for reading instruction," National Institute of Child Health and Human Development, 2000. (pages 7, 9, 24, 30, 32, 43)

M. Orkin et al, "The more you know: How teaching multiple aspects of word knowledge builds fluency skills," *The Reading League Journal*, 3 (2), 2022. (page 4)

C. Perfetti, "Reading ability: Lexical quality to comprehension," *Scientific Studies of Reading*, 11 (4), 2007. (page 30)

P. M. Pexman et al, "There are many ways to be rich: Effects of three measures of semantic richness on visual word recognition," *Psychonomic Bulletin & Review*, 15, 2008. (pages 71, 105, 108)

P. M. Pexman, S. J. Lupker and Y. Hino, "The impact of feedback semantics in visual word recognition: Number-of-features effects in lexical decision and naming tasks," *Psychonomic Bulletin & Review*, 9 (3), 2002. (page 12)

I. Picton, "England's 10-year-olds reach highest ever place in PIRLS international reading rankings," *National Literacy Trust*, 2023. Available at: https://literacytrust.org.uk/blog/englands-10-year-olds-reach-highest-ever-place-in-pirls-international-reading-rankings/ (page 7)

Reading Rockets, "Books for practising letter-sound relationships," Reading Rockets, 2024. Available at: https://www.readingrockets.org/classroom/choosing-and-using-classroom-texts/using-decodable-books (page 15)

Really Great Reading, "Heart Word Magic," Cabin John, MD: Really Great Reading Company, 2024. Available at: https://www.reallygreatreading.com/resources/heart-word-magic (page 44)

D. M. Rehfeld et al, "A meta-analysis of phonemic awareness instruction provided to children suspected of having a reading disability," *Language, Speech, and Hearing Services in Schools*, 53 (4), 2022. (page 24)

H. S. Scarborough, "Connecting early language and literacy to later reading (dis) abilities: Evidence, theory, and practice," in S. Neuman and D. Dickinson, *Handbook for Research in Early Literacy*, Guilford Press, 1, 2001. (pages 9, 54)

M. S. Seidenberg and J. L. McClelland, "A distributed, developmental model of word recognition and naming," *Psychological Review*, 96 (4), 1989. (pages 9, 70)

L. Sibieta, "The crisis in lost learning calls for a massive national policy response," *The Institute for Fiscal Studies*, 2021. Available at: https://ifs.org.uk/articles/crisis-lost-learning-calls-massive-national-policy-response (page 6)

L. Spear-Swerling, *The Structured Literacy Planner: Designing Interventions for Common Reading Difficulties, Grades 1–9*, Guilford Publications, 2024. (page 15)

M. L. Stanback, "Syllable and rime patterns for teaching reading: Analysis of a frequency-based vocabulary of 17,602 words," *Annals of Dyslexia*, 42, 1992. (pages 13, 119–120)

Standards & Testing Agency, "Assessment framework for the development of the year 1 phonics screening check," 2012. Available at: https://www.gov.uk/government/publications/assessment-framework-for-the-development-of-the-year-1-phonics-screening-check/assessment-framework-for-the-development-of-the-year-1-phonics-screening-check (page 67)

K. E. Stanovich, R. G. Nathan and M. Vala-Rossi, "Developmental changes in the cognitive correlates of reading ability and the developmental lag hypothesis," *Reading Research Quarterly*, 21 (3), 1986. (page 15)

The Education Endowment Foundation, "Attendance and reading key barriers to disadvantaged pupils' progress say three in four schools," *The Education Endowment Foundation*, 2025. Available at: https://educationendowmentfoundation.org.uk/news/attendance-and-reading-key-barriers-to-disadvantaged-pupils-progress-say-three-in-four-schools (page 6)

R. Treiman, *Beginning to Spell: A Study of First-Grade Children*, Oxford University Press, 1993. (page 132)

W. E. Tunmer and J. W. Chapman, "The simple view of reading redux: Vocabulary knowledge and the independent components hypothesis," *Journal of Learning Disabilities*, 45 (5), 2012. (page 15)

J. Wanzek et al, "Current evidence on the effects of intensive early reading interventions," *Journal of Learning Disabilities*, 51 (6), 2018. (page 7)

M. Wolf, *Proust and the Squid: The Story and Science of the Reading Brain*, HarperCollins, 2007. (page 7)

M. Wolf, "RAVE-O Instructor Manual Volumes 1 & 2," Frederick, CO: Cambium Learning Group, 2011. (page 8)

M. Wolf, "The Reading Brain: The Canary in the Mind." *Emerging Trends in the Social and Behavioral Sciences: An Interdisciplinary, Searchable, and Linkable Resource*, 2017. (page 9)

M. Wolf et al, "The RAVE-O intervention: Connecting neuroscience to the classroom," *Mind, Brain, and Education*, 3 (2), 2009. (pages 78, 104)

M. Wolf and M. B. Denckla, *RAN/RAS: Rapid Automatized Naming and Rapid Alternating Stimulus Tests*, Austin, TX: Pro-ed, 2005. (page 78)

M. Wolf and T. Katzir-Cohen, "Reading fluency and its intervention," *Scientific Studies of Reading*, 5 (3), 2001. (pages 4, 9, 70)

T. S. Wright and G. N. Cervetti, "A systematic review of the research on vocabulary instruction that impacts text comprehension," *Reading Research Quarterly*, 52 (2), 2017. (pages 92, 107)

M. J. Yap et al, "An abundance of riches: Cross-task comparisons of semantic richness effects in visual word recognition," *Frontiers in Human Neuroscience*, 6, 2012. (page 81)

G. K Zipf, "The meaning-frequency relationship of words," *Journal of General Psychology*, 33, 1945. (page 92)

M. Zipke, L. C. Ehri and H. S. Cairns, "Using semantic ambiguity instruction to improve third graders' metalinguistic awareness and reading comprehension: An experimental study," *Reading Research Quarterly*, 44 (3), 2009. (page 92)

Picture Credits

The publisher would like to thank the following for their kind permission to reproduce their photographs:
(Key: a-above; b-below/bottom; c-centre; f-far; l-left; r-right; t-top)

Sarah Gannon: 191cr; **Alexandria Osburn:** Tim Cameron 191br; **Shutterstock.com:** AboutLife - Raev Denis 155cra, DGLimages 75, fast-stock 58, Grustock 130crb, LightField Studios 106cr, Yuganov Konstantin 123, Med Photo Studio 106tr, MBLifestyle 130cra, Monkey Business Images 80, Kostikova Natalia 81, Okrasiuk 82tr, Orion Production 155cr, PeopleImages.com - Yuri A 26, 76, 93, 100, 140, 166, PHkorsart 82, pics five 176, Alessandro Pintus 40, Rido 18, Studio Romantic 104, Sunny studio 176br

About the Authors

Melissa Orkin is an educator and developmental psychologist who specialises in literacy achievement. Melissa has served as a researcher and instructor at Tufts University. As the director of the educational consulting group Crafting Minds, Melissa collaborates with educators across New England and lives with her family in the Boston area.

Sarah Gannon is a former third grade (Year 4) teacher, reading specialist, literacy coach and Orton-Gillingham practitioner. In her current role as co-director of Crafting Minds, Sarah translates educational research into practical strategies and curriculum resources for teachers. She resides outside of Boston with her husband and three children.

Alexandria Osburn has enjoyed her career as a special educator, reading specialist, literacy coach and Wilson® Dyslexia Practitioner. She is passionate about translating research to practice and creating educator-friendly Structured Literacy resources. Alex lives on Lake Winnipesaukee with her loving husband.

Professional Learning Community Discussion Guide

This guide is designed to support educators in exploring effective literacy instruction strategies and applying them in their classrooms. Each section includes discussion points to encourage collaboration, reflection and actionable steps that give educators the opportunity to exchange insights, address challenges and develop strategies tailored to the unique needs of their learners.

Initial Thoughts	• Which phase of word recognition best aligns with your current small group's reading skills? • Why is it important to integrate often neglected elements of early literacy instruction, including vocabulary, syntax and comprehension? • How might integrating a multi-componential approach represent a shift from current practices?
Chapter 1	• Consider the case of Cameron. How might each Winning Strategy from the chapter support her in moving to the next phase of word reading development? • Which Winning Strategies would you like to integrate into your instruction? • How does backwards planning support a cohesive lesson plan? • How might backwards planning maximise instructional time and pupil achievement?
Chapter 2	• Consider the case of Matteo. How might each Winning Strategy support him in moving to the next phase of word reading development? • How does an approach that emphasises rime patterns support word recognition skills? • For many educators, the Heart Word approach represents a shift from current "tricky word" instruction. What benefits might this approach represent? • Choose 1–2 heart words from a decodable text. Take turns utilising the script to introduce the Heart Word Magic strategy to your colleagues.
Chapter 3	• Consider the case of Sienna. How might each Winning Strategy support Sienna in moving to the next phase of word reading development? • What considerations need to be made when delivering RAN chart instruction to ensure that all pupils are engaged?
Chapter 4	• Consider the case of Jonah. How might each Winning Strategy support Jonah in building stamina with longer words? • What are the benefits of focusing vocabulary instruction on multiple-meaning words? Choose a decodable text and identify multiple-meaning words that lend themselves to this type of instruction.
Chapter 5	• Consider the case of Geoff. How might each Winning Strategy support him in decoding multisyllabic words? • How can teaching single-syllable words utilising a rime pattern approach support accuracy and fluency when reading multisyllabic words? • Consider your experience instructing pupils in syllable types and/or syllable division. What strategies worked well? What challenges have you encountered while teaching this?
Chapter 6	• Consider the cases of Elijah and Nina. How might each Winning Strategy support Elijah and Nina's ability to spell with suffixes? • How does instruction in syntactic knowledge support a multi-componential approach to reading? How might sentence-level comprehension questions support fluency and comprehension?
Chapter 7	• Consider the case of Lee. How might each Winning Strategy support Lee in building sight word recognition with new vowel sounds? • What is both complex and essential about teaching suffixes?
Final Thoughts	• Consider how the template for the Structured Literacy plan has evolved from Chapter 1 to Chapter 5. Make note of strategies that are introduced or faded. How do these adaptations support pupils at various phases of word recognition? How are each of the POSSUM components reinforced? • Choose a decodable book for one of your small groups. Identify the appropriate phase of word reading development. Backwards plan a lesson appropriate for that phase.